"*Lowestoft Chronicle* presents entertaining and exciting stories that lend themselves toward travel without dipping completely over into travel writing." —Kirsten McIlvenna, Newpages.com

"Armchair travelers, rejoice! *Lowestoft Chronicle* brings the far corners of the world to the reader's armchair. The stories and poems vary in tone from dead serious to delightful whimsy, offering something for every taste."
—Mary Beth Magee, Examiner.com

"Travel writers, here's a great place for your work. A tip of the hat (sombrero, fez) to *Lowestoft Chronicle* for fueling our urge to turn off *Jersey Shore*, toss our cell phones into a lake, and go embrace this amazing planet of ours. Bon Voyage!" —Franz Wisner, *New York Times* bestselling author of *Honeymoon with My brother*

"Go ahead, read it right now. I'll wait… Fun, huh? Thought it might pep up your midweek. All things considered, it might just be a very good thing if the *Lowestoft Chronicle* were to achieve their goal of world domination. Best wishes to them!" —Cheryl LaGuardia, *Library Journal*

"Something to check out when you just want to read. They even have a print version…wonderful little collections of short stories and essays. It's worth a look for fans of short stories, creative non-fiction and poetry."
—Dave Dempsey, Radio FM4

"It's unique and the quality of the writing is amazingly high. Highest praise: it made me want to write short stories again."
—Luke Rhinehart, internationally bestselling author of *Matari, Long Voyage Back* and *The Dice Man*

"Full of great talent and exceptionally well written pieces. An entertaining read."  —Tara Smith, *The Review Review* (5-Star Review)

"*Lowestoft Chronicle* is a wonderful new addition to the world of creative writing."   —Tony Perrottet, acclaimed author of *The Naked Olympics*

"A fun read."   —*New York Journal of Books*

"*Lowestoft Chronicle* is a standout among a growing universe of online journals. Every issue delivers a cornucopia of entertaining and thought-provoking stories and articles."  —Michael C. Keith, acclaimed author of
*The Next Better Place*

"A brilliant, savory, sharp, amusing and varied taste of my favorite magazine, *Lowestoft Chronicle*. I'm delighted that a place exists for this kind of travel writing. Nicholas Litchfield has put together something very special, something to celebrate, enjoy, savor."

—Jay Parini, internationally bestselling author of
*The Last Station* and *The Passages of H.M.*

"The *Lowestoft Chronicle* is both classy and fun to read. A work accomplished by careful attention to detail and quality."

—Sheldon Russell, award-winning author of
*Dreams to Dust* and the Hook Runyon mystery series

"Terrific anthology. The writing here is fresh, surprising, and alive. If you aren't familiar with *Lowestoft Chronicle*, head on over there. They publish, on a consistent basis, excellent fiction, poetry, and non-fiction."

—Nicholas Rombes, author of
*A Cultural Dictionary of Punk: 1974-1982*

"I'm always impressed with the quarterly online literary magazine, *Lowestoft Chronicle*—it's filled with intriguing fiction, non-fiction, poetry, and interviews."   —Matthew P. Mayo, Spur Award-winning author of
*Tucker's Reckoning* and *Stranded*

"Nicholas Litchfield's selection of stories, poems, memoirs and interviews is a treasure for readers who enjoy a good dose of humor with their armchair travel." —Mary Donaldson-Evans, author of *Madame Bovary at the Movies* and *Medical Examinations*

"This is the only literary magazine I read these days, and it's always enjoyable. It takes the reader to a wide variety of literary destinations, and makes even a confirmed hermit like me want to get up and go somewhere. Highly recommended." —James Reasoner, *New York Times* bestselling author

"Reading *Lowestoft Chronicle* is like jostling through a sprawling bazaar in Tashkent or Ulaanbaatar, with eyes wide open and wits on high alert. Invigorating, too." —Victor Robert Lee, author of *Performance Anomalies*

"*Lowestoft Chronicle* publishes some of the finest work of travel writing on the Internet today." —Krystal Sierra, *The Review Review* (5-Star Review)

"The much-admired *Lowestoft Chronicle* [is] an eclectic and innovative online journal. Packed into the pages are stories to entice, enthral, and entertain… incisive and enlightening interviews…[and] a tasty blend of pleasing and deftly prepared poems." —Pam Norfolk, *Lancashire Post*

"How did I not know about the *Lowestoft Chronicle*? If you're late to this travel and literary parade as well, check out Nicholas Litchfield's superb online journal specializing in all things to do with travel, literature, and the overlap between these life-nourishing activities."
—James R. Benn, acclaimed author of the Billy Boyle World War II mystery series

"A powerful literary passport—this adventurous anthology is all stamped up with exciting travel-themed writing. With humor, darkness, and charm, its lively prose and poetry will drop you into memorable physical and psychological landscapes. Pack your bags!"
—Joseph Scapellato, acclaimed author of *Big Lonesome*

"The literary equivalent of Rick's Café in *Casablanca*, where travelers of all stripes pull up a stool and swap stories at the bar. Handsomely designed and expertly curated, *Lowestoft Chronicle* drives us into the arms of experience." —Scott Dominic Carpenter, acclaimed author of *Theory of Remainders*

"In this quarterly, you'll find creative nonfiction, short stories, and a few poems, with a welcome dose of humor in many. Wander around the site and you'll find intriguing stories." —Pat Tompkins, Afar.com

"*Lowestoft Chronicle* is contemporary and worldly but with a sepia charm. It's a Baedeker for the vicarious traveler in the age of globalization."
—Ivy Goodman, award-winning author of
*Heart Failure* and *A Chapter from Her Upbringing*

"A solid collection of funny and fine travel-themed stories, poetry, essays and interviews that easily fits in a back pocket or carry-on bag."
— Frank Mundo, Examiner.com

"An impressive collection of travel works that sweeps the reader across the globe. The characters here, though sometimes lost in distant lands and curious customs, never fail to be lost in wonder. Here is your ticket to travel with them, to lose yourself in these pages, to satisfy your inner nomad."
—Dorene O'Brien, award-winning author of
*Voices of the Lost and Found*

"Three attributes of a good literary journal are variety, quality, and the unexpected. *Lowestoft Chronicle* supplies all three."
—Robert Wexelblatt, award-winning author of
*Zublinka Among Women*

"A wonderful collection from a fine literary journal. Fine writing that stirs the imagination, often amuses and always entertains."
—Dietrich Kalteis, award-winning author of
*Ride the Lightning* and *Zero Avenue*

# STEADFAST TREKKERS

A LOWESTOFT CHRONICLE ANTHOLOGY

Books in the Lowestoft Chronicle Anthology Series

LOWESTOFT CHRONICLE 2011 ANTHOLOGY
FAR-FLUNG AND FOREIGN
INTREPID TRAVELERS
SOMEWHERE, SOMETIME...
OTHER PLACES
GRAND DEPARTURES
INVIGORATING PASSAGES
STEADFAST TREKKERS

# STEADFAST TREKKERS

A LOWESTOFT CHRONICLE ANTHOLOGY

EDITED BY NICHOLAS LITCHFIELD

FOREWORD BY ROB DINSMOOR

Lowestoft
Chronicle
Press

# STEADFAST TREKKERS

SUBMISSIONS

The editors welcome submissions of poetry and prose. For submission information please visit our website at www.lowestoftchronicle.com or email: submissions@lowestoftchronicle.com

Copyright © 2018 Lowestoft Chronicle Press
Introduction © 2018 Nicholas Litchfield
Foreword © 2018 Rob Dinsmoor
Additional copyright information can be found on pages 225-228.

All rights reserved. No part of this book may be used or reproduced in any manner whatsoever without written permission from the publisher except in the case of brief quotations embodied in critical articles and reviews. For information, contact
editor@lowestoftchronicle.com
Published by Lowestoft Chronicle Press, Cambridge, Massachusetts
www.lowestoftchronicle.com

First edition: September 2018

Cover and book design by Tara Litchfield

ISBN 13: 978-1-7323328-0-5
ISBN 10: 1-7323328-0-0

Printed in the United States of America

# CONTENTS

Foreword / Rob Dinsmoor     11
Introduction / Nicholas Litchfield     13

## FICTION

On the Oxford to York / Arianna S. Warsaw-Fan Rauch     19
One Star / Sharon Frame Gay     37
Rome 1973 / Todd McKie     47
La Tomatina / Robert Mangeot     53
Holy Water / Karen Fayeth     76
Hsi-Wei and the Good / Robert Wexelblatt     80
Whose Fault? / Lenny Levine     90
A World of Eternal Silence / Alistair Rey     109
Emily / Elaine Barnard     120
What Do Mares Eat? / Rob Dinsmoor     136
The Man With No Outlines / Tushar Jain     157
Farmer Joe / Ruyi Wen     183
Dream Job / AN Block     199

## POETRY

Traveling Companion / Mary Beth Magee     26
Chariot / Tamra Plotnick     52
R.O.T. Rallies / Jill Hawkins     65
Manna / Kenneth P. Gurney     75
Strangers on a Train / James B. Nicola     99
The Mystery of the Stairs / George Moore     117
The Taxi I Called / Saundra Norton     145
Self-Portrait / Richard Luftig     155
Hitchhiker / Joe Albanese     178

## INTERVIEW

| | |
|---|---|
| The Return of the Railroad Bull: | |
| A Conversation with Sheldon Russell | 29 |
| A Conversation with Dietrich Kalteis | 192 |

## CREATIVE NON-FICTION

| | |
|---|---|
| Sarge / Michael C. Keith | 43 |
| Angie's Wedding / Charles Joseph Albert | 58 |
| Bite Me / Jeanine Pfeiffer | 66 |
| The Sweetest Sound / Mary Donaldson-Evans | 100 |
| The Acute and the Grave / Scott Dominic Carpenter | 113 |
| Massaged in Vein / Sabrina Harris | 130 |
| A Daihatsu Doctor / Roland Barnes | 140 |
| Japanese Taxis and Elementary Incidents / Anthony Head | 146 |
| Musical Chairs at Larksome Lodge / Olga Pavlinova Olenich | 166 |
| Lost and Found in Russia / Judy S. Richardson | 171 |
| The Vomit Comet To Koh Tao / Brennen Fahy | 179 |
| The Paperboy Incident / Frank Morelli | 205 |

**CONTRIBUTORS** | 215
**COPYRIGHT NOTES** | 225
**ACKNOWLEDGEMENTS** | 229

# FOREWORD

Rob Dinsmoor

When I read, I want to be taken somewhere I've never been before. This is what drew me into reading and writing in the first place. Too often in literary magazines these days, the focus is on realism, as if the purpose of writing is to mimic everyday life so that everything is comfortable and familiar to us, reaffirming our view of the world and our place in it. Travel stories in particular often focus only on the ideal vacation, enjoying sumptuous food among wonderful and fascinating people, free from worry, a photo album's worth of great scenery and pleasant activities that are fun for the whole family. *Lowestoft Chronicle* provides none of these comforts.

When we travel, we're leaving ordinary life behind us. We deal with all kinds of challenges in the form of less-than-ideal lodging, strange food, questionable transportation, language and cultural barriers, and our sometimes difficult fellow travelers.

I've taken in some breathtaking views in the U.S., Mexico, Central America, Europe, and New Zealand, but what I remember most fondly are the adventures: That crazy, reckless taxi driver in Belize who had removed the seat belts from his cab. Landing in a Guadeloupe airport next to a crashed, incinerated plane that no one had bothered to haul off. Inadvertently kayaking too close to the gators in the Everglades. Awaking to howler monkeys at a yoga retreat in Costa Rica and coming home with a particularly nasty case of Giardia. Trying to figure out the instructions on an ATM machine in Guatemala while being watched by a guard armed with a machine gun. That scorpion on the breakfast table at the five-star resort. Wheeling suitcases two miles down a long, hilly, winding road at night in Volterra, due to a series of miscalculations.

Without these adventures, we would have no stories to tell when we get back home. Instead, as others often do, we would bore our friends with only a laundry list of cities we visited, restaurants where we dined and what we ate there, and impressive hotels where we lodged.

All stories and poems in *Lowestoft Chronicle* are, in a broad sense, travel adventures. Some take us to places we'll likely never to have the fortune—or misfortune—to visit. Others transport us through time. Some examine foreign cultures from within, sometimes from the point of view of an entrenched outsider. Others coax us into unsettling situations. Some take us to imaginary places and situations that have rules and logic of their own. The interviews guide us through the fertile minds of established writers and rising stars.

As you embark on the destinations in this anthology, fasten your seatbelt—if you have one—and hold onto your seat.

# INTRODUCTION
Nicholas Litchfield

Embarking on an extensive slog of overseas travel can be a daunting, stressful business, especially when faced with a different language, different currency and customs. These exciting, enlightening, and rejuvenating excursions, while they might be good for the soul, wreak havoc on one's bank account. And then there are all those other things to fret about, like scorpions, spies, terrorists, gigolos, and sadistic masseuses giving you a rough rubdown because you pointed at the wrong thing on the menu board. Peculiarly, the strangers you meet seem genuinely concerned about your safety, but, alas, instead of a handshake, they kiss you excessively on each of your rosy red cheeks. Be that as it may, the good thing about travel is that it provides one with some remarkable travel tales—the sort of offbeat, perceptive, spirited writing that feel right at home in *Lowestoft Chronicle*.

In *Steadfast Trekkers*, the seventh volume in our mixed-form anthology series, there is the customary cocktail of exquisite poetry and colorful prose. Full of fascinating settings and intriguing situations, the following pieces are rich with humor, drama and mishap, and a healthy dose of community spirit.

In two absorbing Indonesia-set travelogues, villagers come to the aid of Jeanine Pfeiffer, a foreign scientist stung by a scorpion in "Bite Me," and in "Massaged in Vein," Sabrina Harris bravely suffers a traditional vein massage. In Robert Wexelblatt's "Hsi-Wei and the Good," a perceptive vagabond poet is able to use his connections to alleviate taxation burdens on the poor. In "Emily" by Elaine Barnard, a scholarship student overcomes discrimination at a university in China, and in Karen Fayeth's "Holy Water," a priest strives to save his parish as raging fires consume San Francisco.

Elsewhere, the tension and anxiety is thick in Judith S. Richardson's "Lost and Found in Russia" and "Angie's Wedding" by Charles Joseph Albert. As a guest lecturer in Russia for a month, Richardson stealthily navigates her way around frosty Moscow and Saint Petersburg, keen to make it home in one piece, and Albert, an anxious Texan, wonders which family member will be the first to embarrass his sister at her chic wedding in Provence.

The poems in Steadfast Trekkers explore the advantages, pleasures, and hardships of life on the road, fear of going someplace new, and a cautionary note about not opening one's eyes to the beauty around us. Joe Albanese gives the thumbs up to the unburdened, eternal wanderer in "Hitchhiker," and George Moore's "The Mystery of the Stairs" gives the thumbs-down to change and the unfamiliar. While in Richard Luftig's "Self-Portrait," a well-traveled man is so focused on his camera and his Facebook profile that he neglects the natural and man-made wonders in front of him.

The outlandish and the offbeat have a habit of working their way into the mix. Among the highlights: when a frazzled, work-shy salesman switches companies and falls into the role of confidant and quasi-therapist to work colleagues, he finds his new role almost as draining and stressful as his previous job, in AN Block's laugh-out-loud story "Dream Job." Todd McKie's "Rome 1973" is a wild romance about a newly graduated American art student and his exciting, though fleeting, affair with a volatile Italian dominatrix. And in the satirical "Farmer Joe," Ruyi Wen uncovers a disturbing link between organic soybeans and anti-American terrorists.

Whether traveling on foot or by car, plane, train, or by motorbike, those we encounter on the way to our destination many times enhance our memory of the trip. In the case of the thankful hiker in Kenneth P. Gurney's "Manna," passersby lift his spirits when they provide him with an unexpected thirst quencher on his wearying journey through the wilderness. In Mary Beth Magee's spiritually uplifting "Traveling Companion," a long-departed relative accompanies the lone traveler on her lengthy train ride. And in Jill Hawkins' "R.O.T. Rallies" those from all walks of life band together like family at a motorcycle rally in Austin, united by the powerful engine between their thighs.

Sometimes one's interactions with fellow travelers can be about as pleasant as a bout of turbulence. The flier wedged between an obnoxious chatterbox and a beautiful but petrified woman in Lenny Levine's "Whose Fault?" experiences pleasure and pain in equal measure. A morbid old woman who, on a wearisome train journey through the gloomy English countryside exhausts a young stranger with countless tales of gruesome local tragedy in the splendidly comic "On the Oxford to York" by Arianna S. Warsaw-Fan Rauch. And in James B. Nicola's breezy poem "Strangers on a Train," a surly non-English speaking local spoils a tourist's peace and tranquility.

Language difficulties are further explored, and to humorous effect. Mary Donaldson-Evans' lighthearted essay "The Sweetest Sound" is an entertaining account of her travels through southern Africa. Scott Dominic Carpenter, in his devilishly funny "The Acute and the Grave," playfully explores language and accent difficulties in France. "Chariot," the witty poem by Tamra Plotnick, looks at relationships and the language of love—a language that is, regrettably, perpetually confusing to most of us. In Alistair Rey's "A World of Eternal Silence," the emphasis is on a different means of communication—that of visual gestures and signs—as, amid the glorious sounds of a symphonic ensemble, a news reporter in London investigates the education of those enrolled in a school for the deaf.

In sharp contrast, the narrator in Rob Dinsmoor's mesmerizing "What Do Mares Eat?" tormented by a song from his youth playing endlessly in his head. Later, we encounter another tormented soul, a blurry, formless man on a park bench in Mumbai in Tushar Jain's uniquely surreal "The Man With No Outlines." Afflicted by a strange condition that has destroyed his life, the sorrowful tale he recounts to a passing mathematician has unsettling repercussions.

"Musical Chairs at Lakshmi Lodge," also set in India, is an entertaining piece by frequent *Lowestoft Chronicle* contributor Olga Pavlinova Olenich. In this travel tale, she focuses her attention on an unfortunate incident with a plastic chair and young Casanovas who make a habit of wooing mature women.

In other travel-related pieces, the topic of taxicabs and automobile troubles arise. Longtime expatriate Anthony Head relates his many fascinating and peculiar experiences in "Japanese Taxis and Elementary Incidents." A rider finds herself in an embarrassing situation in Saundra Norton's witty "The Taxi I Called," and Roland Barnes' delightful "A Daihatsu Doctor" charts the breakdowns of a car named Rocky and the healing powers of a former Gran Prix mechanic.

Robert Mangeot's latest work, "La Tomatina," presents an itinerant American exploring the more desirable parts of Europe. Here, an aging wife with pent-up grievances toward her husband finds therapeutic reward from a world-famous food fight festival in eastern Spain. Armed with tomatoes, and bearing a determined glint in her eye, the messy sporting spectacle allows her a moment of cathartic release.

There is release of a different sort in Brennen Fahy's comically graphic "The Vomit Comet To Koh Tao," as a rough ferry ride in Thailand turns into a chaotic journey of misery and despair for returning partygoers. While in the funny, nostalgic "The Paperboy Incident," Frank Morelli takes us to Jersey Shore in the summer of 1985, where a restless seven-year-old struggles to contain himself as he awaits his first encounter with a hot new arcade game.

It's not all fun and games, of course. Some of the more poignant pieces include well-told fictional and autobiographical narratives spotlighting servicemen on active duty—Michael C. Keith recollects his days at a missile base in Korea in 1962 in "Sarge," and in Sharon Frame Gay's "One Star," we encounter a young soldier stranded on a life raft during WWII.

Included in this anthology is an interview with Dietrich Kalteis, winner of an Independent Publisher Book Award for his debut novel and author of four subsequent well-praised books. A gritty writer of fast-paced crime stories who, according to the *Globe and Mail* "celebrates machismo in all its tough and tawdry glory," Kalteis is rapidly emerging as one of Canada's top modern crime writers. Here, he discusses his writing, his influences, and his most recent novel, *Zero Avenue*, which is a gangland drug tale set in Vancouver in 1979, featuring a tough female punk singer.

There is also an interview with Sheldon Russell, an award-winning author of historical fiction and a Spur-award finalist. In this, his second interview with *Lowestoft Chronicle*, Russell discusses his work in progress, his writing process, as well as the latest book in his famous Hook Runyon mystery series.

*Steadfast Trekkers* is dedicated to those valiant travelers craving new experiences who are willing to forgo comfort, ease, and restful retreats for an unforgettable stretch of heady adventure. And though, at times, we may pity the forlorn tourists who endure rough journeys by land, sea, or air, and encounter trouble and strife in strange foreign lands, it is hard not to relish their misfortunes and savor their colorful, captivating tales. Your woe was worth it, one wants to tell them…it provided us with a great deal of entertainment. Muchas gratias and long may your wanderings continue.

# ON THE OXFORD TO YORK
Arianna S. Warsaw-Fan Rauch

Cedric Blake had taken the train from Oxford to York nearly ten times during his first two years at university, but he'd never realized how many tragedies had occurred along its tracks until he'd had the pleasure of sitting across from Cynthia Mott, an elderly woman who seemed to have spent her three-hundred-or-so years on the planet cataloging every misfortune that had occurred in England from the days of the Norman Dynasty up until the present—and earmarking, for future conversational use, the most horrific and gruesome of the lot.

Her morbid dispatches ran—like a news ticker—without pause and were made all the more absurd by the fact that she carried with her a small teddy bear, which sat upright in her lap and stared unapologetically across the table at Cedric. Perhaps, he mused, its name was Aloysius. They *were* traveling from Oxford, after all.

Between the bear and her shapeless, too-large frock, this elderly Mott had the overall appearance of an eerie little girl who'd dropped by the dining room to say goodnight to the adults before heading off to bed. Cedric only knew that she was old because of her wrinkled face and the fact that she wore nylons—in spite of the heat—just like his grandmother.

"Oh dear," she sighed, glancing sadly out over the passing landscape. "It must have been around here, mustn't it?"

Cedric was silent. He'd been drifting in and out of sleep for the past five minutes, and although he had, indeed, been awake for this last interruption, his shuttered eyelids, which were careful to betray not even a flicker of life, seemed to him to provide a very suitable excuse for absenting himself from the conversation.

"It was before your time, of course," continued this Miss or Ms. or Mrs. Mott, undeterred by his silence. "It was a great fire, you see. Very sad. All of those people burnt to ashes."

He suspected that she was looking at him—scanning him for signs of consciousness—but he remained resolutely still. It wasn't that he didn't *care* about the factory workers who'd died of tuberculosis all of those years ago—or the children who'd drowned in their local well—or the sad woman who was said to have thrown herself off the highest tower of some castle near Birmingham way back in the 17th century. It's just that he wished he didn't know about them. Because he liked to be happy, you see—and consequently, he'd always kept his knowledge of such tragedies to a minimum. He knew about the Battle of Agincourt—and the murders of Jack the Ripper—but that was about the extent of it.

Was that so very awful? *Not at all*, he answered himself. If anything, it was a sign of his considerable compassion. Perhaps this *Mott* character could sit there and chat casually about the brutal murder of a sixteen-year-old girl, but *he* was far too empathetic. He was also too tired—because last night's end-of-term bash had taken it out of him somewhat.

Thankfully, his companion seemed to have accepted the premise that he was asleep—for her voice faded gradually into a whisper—and soon it was undetectable over the grinding and squeaking of the wheels on the tracks. That was big of her, thought Cedric, as he fell further out of consciousness. She'd shown him much more respect than he'd shown her. But there would be plenty of time for politeness later—because she, too, was riding all the way to York. She'd mentioned that in her opening introductions—along with the fact that she liked Marmalade—but not if it had ginger in it—and that her shoes had orthopedic inserts—and that her three cats were staying with her friend Gertrude while she was away for the weekend. Still, what would she do in his conversational absence? Read about a particularly gruesome witch-burning? Knit a decorative noose for her boudoir?

Through the flickering gap between his upper and lower lids, he could see her pointing out the window and tracing a path through the quaint scenery. Perhaps she was mapping the route of some wrongfully-convicted, escaped prisoner who'd perished on his way to freedom. She was fiddling with something, too—with her other hand. Her locket. He'd noticed it hanging low about her neck when he'd first gotten on the train, but he'd averted his eyes when he'd realized where he was looking. *"So that's what you like, is it?"* he could almost hear his girlfriend Anna teasing. *"Dentures and shriveled baps?"* He'd met Anna just over a year ago—at the end of his second term. She was at Somerville College and she was coming to meet his parents in just a few weeks.

———— ✦ ————

Cedric must have fallen asleep after that because he woke up sometime later, vaguely aware of having dreamt about a fire—and a steak and ale pie. His mother was making one for his welcome-home dinner that evening.

"Hungry, dear?" asked a voice.

Cedric started and blinked groggily at Ms. Mott. Had he mumbled something in his sleep?

"I went to the restaurant car," she said. "I brought you a few sandwiches and some crisps in case you were. I wasn't sure what you liked."

"Oh, I—er, thank you," he said.

It had been ages since a stranger had offered him food. He hadn't known that it was still a done thing. But she seemed so pleased with her efforts—and the sandwiches were still wrapped—and, after all, he *was* a bit hungry. So, he sat there nibbling and making unintelligent comments about the weather and the scenery and so forth—and whenever they passed by the site of a particularly grisly death, his companion informed him of the fact and offered a few details by way of commemoration. Cedric had accepted this. He'd started to find it rather hilarious, actually, now that he was rested. In just a few hours, he'd be laughing about it with his mum and dad over a plate of pie—and anything that happened between now and then would only enrich the story he'd have to tell—about the batty old lady on the train.

"Oh—Sheffield," said the old bat now, shaking her head sadly. "Dear me, dear me. Those poor people. And so many of them, too. Crushed to death, when all they wanted was to see a game."

"You mean, at Hillsborough stadium?" asked Cedric. He'd heard about *that*, of course. His club was Manchester United—and Old Trafford had hosted the second semi-finals that year between Liverpool and Nottingham Forest after the first match was called off due to the crush.

She nodded at him solemnly, suddenly quiet. This surprised him. He'd expected her to pounce on his sudden responsiveness—to seize the opportunity to discuss one of her beloved catastrophes. But she seemed focused on something else now. She was staring distractedly out the window. And she was fiddling about with her locket again.

———— ✦ ————

Ten minutes passed in silence. Practically an eternity in the context of this train ride. Then Ms. Mott spoke.

"There," she said, pointing to a hill and craning her neck, as if she could almost see it, "Just behind there. That's where I lost my Tommy."

Cedric froze. He swallowed the kind of dry swallow that always made him have to do it again.

"I'm—I'm sorry," he stammered. "Was he your—?"

"My son," she said.

"When?" he asked hoarsely, barely able to articulate himself. He felt as if a giant melon-baller had plunged itself into his torso and hollowed him out. This had been a comedy—a scene from a Dürrenmatt play. But, suddenly, the lens of humor had vanished and everything about the situation and their surroundings seemed oppressively sad.

"Oh, years ago," she said. "I'm going to visit him now."

Cedric pictured her, bending unsteadily over Tommy's grave, resting the small teddy bear up against the headstone. It made sense now, her need to collect tragedies. Perhaps it gave her strength to know how many people had faced sadness before and come out of it. Or maybe their stories gave her a sense of belonging—of companionship.

"Do you want to see a picture of him?" she asked.

She opened her locket and held it up for Cedric to see. He leaned forward.

"He was six in that photo—it was taken just days before I lost him."

"I—I can't imagine," said Cedric. "I'm—"

He broke off, unsure of what to say. In his own short life, he'd never faced anything to compare with her loss. And he felt horribly ashamed of himself for having thought her ridiculous. His face burned and tears of sympathy and self-loathing sprang to his eyes.

"My dear boy!" cried Mrs. Mott. "Are you quite well? There's no need to look so glum! I found him again a few hours later! I should have mentioned that, I suppose. It was terrifying, of course. I mean, I spent half the day thinking that I'd lost my little boy. But then, there he was. He'd tumbled down the hill, you see—without making a peep—or hurting himself—and then made himself at home behind a pile of rocks. He's all grown up now—with kids and everything."

She held up the teddy bear and waved it at him as if to say "why else would I have this thing with me?"

Cedric, who'd been holding his breath throughout her explanation, exhaled now—forcefully. He was almost shaking with relief. But Cynthia Mott, who seemed completely unaware of the ordeal she'd just put him through, went prattling on about how it had all happened—about what Tommy had been wearing and why—and about how steep the fall was, and how jagged the rocks were, and how lucky he was to have missed them. It took until the end of her story for Cedric's heart rate to return to its normal tempo.

"So, you see," she said in conclusion, "Whenever I come here, I always have to think about all of the awful things that took place along this line, and about how Tommy's death was almost one of them. It makes me so grateful for the life I've had."

She smiled at him warmly, her wrinkles folding into larger wrinkles. And Cedric smiled back.

For the last few minutes of the journey, they chatted about Anna and Cedric's family—and Ms. Mott told him about her love of history and about how she'd moved to Oxford to live with an Indian man she'd met while they were both on holiday in Cornwall. She came back to visit her grandchildren every month and had a little tea shop on Pembroke street, which she'd opened about ten years ago. Cedric should stop by with his friends sometime, she said; she made curry scones every Wednesday.

Eventually, they reached their stop, and Cedric helped to carry her bags off the train. When they parted ways at the station, he wished her well and promised to visit her soon. She assured him that Tommy and his family were waiting just outside to pick her up—and that there was no need for him to escort her any further. He watched her as she tottered away, her fragile form growing smaller in the distance.

She turned to wave at him just as his parents came over to greet him.

"Who's that?" asked his mother.

"A teacher—from Oxford," he said, smiling.

He would tell them about the shop and the curry scones later on.

# TRAVELING COMPANION
Mary Beth Magee

I hand my bag up
Into the care of a handsome porter.
He places it behind him on the floor of the railroad car
And turns back to offer his hand to me.
A queen for a moment, I accept his help
With a gracious nod
And step up into my royal coach,
A silver sleeper car on twin steel tracks.
The pressure of a hand on my back aids my ascent.
When I turn to thank my helper,
No one is behind me.
The ebony porter questions me with a look.
"Thank you" seems little enough to say
But I say it anyway
And smile an apology for my delay.
His answering grin lights up the shadowed vestibule.
He points me to my compartment,
An upholstered closet which will be my home-
At least for the next few days.
As I try to slide the door shut, I feel it stick.
A moment later, the resistance fades
And I can close the panel.
Now I understand.
The hand on my back,
The push on the door-
My traveling companion has joined me.

Granddaddy was a railroad man.
He died beneath the wheels of a train,
Crushed and severed by cold steel
Meeting warm flesh in the night.
"His lantern went out" was the explanation.
"The engineer thought he had the go-ahead signal."
In those days before electronic communications,
Men lived and died by the amount of fuel in their lanterns.
And Granddaddy was one who died.

I never met him.
His fatal sojourn took place years before I was born.
Yet I feel him with me whenever I board a train.
As a child, I received endless fussing over-
From train personnel who had known him-
Whenever my grandmother and I traveled by train.
What does a toddler know of dead ancestors?
I only knew I felt at home on those old trains,
And sensed myself well loved by those I met.
Those days ended too soon
As school schedules and changes in railway rules
Put train rides on the back burner of my life.

Now I ride with greater understanding of the magic.
This ticket, paid for from my funds,
Carries me across the country
Not just a state line.
Heading out on an adventure of hope
Or joy or desperation, I ride the train.
I do not ride alone.

I look out of windows at scenes Granddaddy might have seen,
Rock to the same rhythm he felt,
Listen to the steady rumble of the wheels.

Does it make him smile to know
His love of the rails runs in my veins?
Is the thrill I feel when I hear the cry of a lonesome train whistle
Pierce the dark velvet of the night
An echo of his feelings?

The miles sweep by, telephone poles and backs of towns
Interspersed with trees and fields.
Trestles transport us across rivers and streams.
We skirt glittering lakes.
The sun sets and nighttime's blanket shakes out
A pattern of stars streaking high above the dark ground.
The throbbing locomotive draws me closer to my destination
And the loss of this connection to my spiritual traveling companion.
When I disembark from the time machine which is a train,
I leave him behind.
Does he ride the rails and watch for my return?
Or is he drawn back to this world only
When I connect to his?

# THE RETURN OF THE RAILROAD BULL: A CONVERSATION WITH SHELDON RUSSELL
*Lowestoft Chronicle* (December 2017)

Versatile, award-winning novelist Sheldon Russell is the author of ten published works of fiction, ranging from American frontier novels and tales of the Oklahoma Land Rush, to postwar mysteries and a fictional account of Francisco Vázquez Coronado's 1540s North American expedition. A finalist for Best Original Paperback in the 2001 Western Writers of America, Inc. Spur Awards competition, and winner of the Langum Prize for Excellence in American Historical Fiction, Russell is best known for his critically acclaimed Hook Runyon historical mystery series.

Dr. Sheldon Russell
(Photography: Bob Bozarth/Bozarth Photography, Guthrie, OK)

His credible, hardboiled central character, a one-armed railroad bull named Hook, and colorful, fully fleshed supporting cast have earned him starred reviews from *Publishers Weekly* and *Booklist*. Newspapers like *The New York Times*, the *San Francisco Chronicle*, and *The Denver Post* have praised him for his thrilling action, suspenseful storylines, historical background details, and insights into railroad life. Two of the books in the series were chosen as finalists for the Oklahoma

Book Award competition, and one was selected by *Publishers Weekly* as one of the six best mysteries of the year.

After 2013's *The Hanging of Samuel Ash*, the positively reviewed fourth Hook mystery, the series came to an unexpected halt. Now, at long last, the railroad bull has returned, and the latest mystery, his most challenging to date, proves to be his best adventure yet.

In an exclusive interview with *Lowestoft Chronicle*, Russell discusses his new Hook Runyon novel and some of the supporting characters, as well as several of his previous books and works in progress.

**Lowestoft Chronicle (LC)**: In the latest Hook Runyon Mystery, *The Bridge Troll Murders*, Hook goes undercover as a hobo in an effort to catch a serial killer preying on freighthopping vagrants. *The Insane Train* (book #2) deservedly earned glowing reviews from major review sites, including *The New York Times*, but I think this fifth series entry may well be the standout book in the series. Did the novel take shape from the initial idea of a serial killer or stem from a desire to send Hook far beyond Oklahoma and experience again his old life as a train-hopping vagrant?

**Sheldon Russell (SR)**: My wife is a sculptor, and we had restored an old 1893 building, converting it into a studio and gallery with a Victorian apartment on the upper floor. The old commercial building was only yards from the railroad tracks, and trains roared by day and night. Shortly after we moved in, a number of random and brutal killings took place across the U.S, all within walking distance of the tracks. The murderer was eventually dubbed the railway killer by the press. Trains would often stop at the crossing below our window at night, and I remember lying there, wondering whether or not the killer might be getting off the train that very moment. That feeling of vulnerability was the impetus for *The Bridge Troll*

*Murders*. Only after I was into the book did I realize that it was, in large part, the randomness of the crimes that was so terrifying and made capture so difficult. The only plausible thing left to do was to set a trap. Who better for bait than an old hobo like Hook Runyon?

**LC**: In the book, you allow the reader a fascinating peek at hobo culture, exploring things like Hobo Code of Ethics and hobo hieroglyphics. And through Hook, we get a sense of what established hobo "jungles" were like and some of the common perils of riding the rails (such as being trapped in boxcars). How extensive was your research into the language, attitudes, and lifestyle of traveling vagrants in the postwar period?

**SR**: I do a fair amount of research and rather enjoy it. In fact, I've had to limit how much I do in order to have time to write. I'm forever looking at systems maps to determine what rail lines go where and when they were built. Then there's the whole business of engine types and what was running when and how many drive wheels they had, and don't forget the rail hobbyist, who pride themselves on railroad minutiae.

The hobo communication system that you speak of has been in existence for decades, though I do find variations from one railroad to the next and in different parts of the country. Most of the signs and symbols hoboes left behind communicated where the safe houses were, who would give out good food, even what houses should be avoided. I discovered along the way any number of railroad slang lists, compiled in large part by railroaders themselves, they being renowned for their use of nicknames for just about everything. While I had great fun with this, I did learn to curb myself in order to avoid having to construct cumbersome glossaries.

Of course, it doesn't hurt that I grew up in a railroad town, that my father was a machinist for the Santa Fe, and that our school song was *I've Been Working on the Railroad*. So, I could hardly have avoided any of it, even if I had wanted. I am most grateful for having known these men and for being exposed to their wisdom and humor.

**LC**: One of the many enjoyable things about this novel is the reappearance of moonshiner Runt Wallace, a character from the first Hook Runyon mystery. You had mentioned in our previous interview in 2014 that Runt would return, but, nevertheless, when he does appear it's rather unexpected. Why did you decide to impose significant changes to his life and why relocate him? Will he emerge again in future books?

**SR**: I hadn't necessarily planned on bringing Runt back so soon, but my readers had different ideas. And the truth is that I missed him myself. There is an innocence about Runt, I think, that softens the hardness of the times and the tougher side of Hook as well. It's great fun playing them off each other, and it's through their repartee that the depth of their relationship is best revealed. Runt's life-changes reflect what had happened to so many families after the war, particularly in Oklahoma, where farms had failed and so many men had been lost to the war. New and more liberal laws had decimated moonshining as a profitable business, leaving Runt to struggle for a living. The notion of Hook and Runt meeting up on the road appealed to me. Coincidence can be delightful in a story, if not abused. Runt's my kind of guy, and I expect to see him again in the future.

**LC**: Ria Wolfe, a Boston University Ph.D. student studying forensic psychology, serves as a highly effective character in the book, not solely studying crime scenes to develop a criminal profile, but also analyzing Hook and his methods. In *The Yard Dog*, you mention that Hook was "neither trained for nor inclined to law enforcement" but "discovered a propensity for the work." How would you describe Hook's methods? How did he become a Santa Fe bull?

**SR**: Under different circumstances, Hook most likely would not have been hired as a Santa Fe bull. But, having lost an arm, he was ineligible for the draft during the war, and the railroad was desperate for men. The fact that he was a well-seasoned hobo was, ironically, an asset when it came to enforcing the law on the rails. Hook is infinitely logical and practical in his approach to solving crime. He does what works and has little patience for contemplating why criminals behave as they do. He's quick to drop the hat and does not abide fools. His past experiences as a hobo serve him well in the rough and tumble world of railroad bulls. While honest and trustworthy for the most part, he is not above bending the rules from time to time and has an acquired taste for busthead liquor and book collecting.

**LC**: The book collecting aspect is an interesting trait of Hook's. As you point out in *The Bridge Troll Murders*, it has gone beyond a passion and now verges on an obsession. Hook collects everything from fiction and biographies to travel and religious books, although he doesn't read everything he buys. He values signed first editions over anything else, and even when ravenously hungry he would rather choose a first edition book over a meal. First of all, why did you make him a book fanatic? And why the decision not to narrow his reading interests?

**SR**: I'm a believer in the notion that intelligence is where you find it, and I wanted to demonstrate this by showing Hook's innate cleverness and curiosity about the world this way. For him to pursue knowledge through academic pursuit struck me as contrary to who he is and the way that he lives. Collecting books, however, is concrete. It gives him not only intellectual stimulation but has monetary value as well, which makes it an okay thing for him to do.

Ria's intelligence, which is formal, research-based, and equally formidable, provides a handy counterbalance and contrast.

**LC**: In this latest book, Hook has been promoted to assistant division supervisor of security. Eddie Preston, the division supervisor out of Chicago, has little respect for Hook and tried to prevent him being hired in the first place. Why did you decide to promote Hook? Will this new responsibility have an impact in later books?

**SR**: Hook's boss, Eddie Preston, has reluctantly offered the job because he found himself in a manpower bind. While Hook has considered taking the promotion, he is clearly not suited for a desk job. On top of that, in the meantime, he's managed to burn up half the countryside and a perfectly good railroad bridge. I'm thinking Eddie might reconsider the offer. If he doesn't, Hook probably will.

**LC**: Typically, how long does it take you to write a Hook mystery? Are you working from an outline and are they written from beginning to end?

**SR**: A year, if all goes well and the world lets me. Under the best of circumstances, I like a few months for a manuscript to cool off before I begin my revisions. There's just nothing like time to bring real objectivity to the task. I do a rough outline of the entire manuscript first to get a general direction and an idea for the conclusion. To me, all stories are journeys. Once I know what the journey is, I can then outline each chapter before I write it, some of it little more than brainstorming. If I come up with a better idea while writing, out it goes. Nothing or no one is sacred. I write from beginning to end, often rewriting the first chapter after I'm finished. I find this helps me clear out back-story and begin the tale where it counts.

**LC**: Am I correct in thinking *The Bridge Troll Murders* was written in 2013? I recall you once saying that you had an attic full of unpublished novels, suggesting that you are a productive writer. Have you been working on numerous Hook mysteries during the past three years or concentrating on different projects?

**SR**: Finished, in part at that time, as I recall, though I've slept since then. I usually have several projects going at once. Sometimes I'll set a manuscript aside if I come up against a problem that I can't solve. I'm a big believer in sleeping on things and letting the subconscious do its business. I've been working on a book that is known paradoxically as autobiographical fiction. It has a working title of *A Particular Madness*. It's not an easy book to write, since I have to take a pretty hard look at myself. Sometimes there are things I'd rather not see.

**LC**: In our previous interview, you mentioned you were working on several other novels (*The Woodcutter*, *Blood Rights*, and *Shrink Wrapped*). Did you complete those novels, and are you actively seeking publication for them?

**RS**: These books are complete, having undergone finite revisions and some title changes. They represent my interests in historic frontier subjects and psychological thrillers. All are currently out and about looking for a way to publication. I do not have a literary agent, do not live in the cultural center of the world, and am better equipped to write than I am to agent.

**LC**: You had great success a number of years ago with some thrilling and moving American frontier novels featuring the U.S. Cavalry doctor McReynolds. His mixed-blood son Creed later surfaced as one of your characters. Why did you continue the McReynolds saga? Are there other periods in history you're interested in writing about?

**RS**: I needed to bring Creed back to the frontier as an educated man in the second book, not only to demonstrate his success as a modern man but also to show how his earlier world had changed. I wanted this kind of closure for him and for the readers of the saga.

My parents were poor Okies during the Great Depression and Dust Bowl days of the thirties. I think I have some insight into those times and have always wanted to write about that period. Steinbeck is pretty tough competition, however.

**LC**: Rumor has it the next Hook adventure might be published as early as fall of 2018. Is the novel completed and are you able to talk about it?

**SR**: While I don't control the publishing schedule, it is my understanding that there may well be a 2018 Hook book. The manuscript is in rough draft form and with a working title of *Evil Rides A Train*. After the war, the world was in chaos and bursting with war orphans. Nowhere was this more evident than in Germany and Poland. With no place else to go after the war, many of these orphans were put in the same concentration camps where their parents had been killed. Hook is charged with moving these orphans across the country and must struggle with the forces of good and evil.

# ONE STAR
Sharon Frame Gay

All I need is one star to guide me. Doesn't matter where it swims in the sky. It's enough if it pokes through the clouds and keeps me company.

I've been on this raft for days now. Lost count a while back when I fell into such a deep sleep that I may have been unconscious for hours, bobbing along in the middle of the sea like a sad little cork that forgot to stay in the bottle.

Getting shot down was like shoving your head up a Banshee's ass. The sound and fury of hurtling toward earth wipes out any common sense a person might have, replacing it with screams for our mothers, our girlfriends, our God.

"Milo, get ready for impact," shouted Captain Walker, our pilot, pulling up on the joystick as though terror could change the course of gravity.

The other guys were screaming and tumbling about the plane. I sat there like a deer caught in the headlights, adding to the cries that painted the inside of our bomber, soon to be brushed again with splatters of blood and urine and body parts that stuck to the fuselage. Barnacles of death on a silver bullet.

Was it luck that we hit the water instead of land? You might think so. Another fifteen miles and we might have buried ourselves in some tropical forest. Hitting the water gave the few of us who survived the impact a fighting chance.

"Milo, over here!" someone shouted, and I saw Arnie kicking at the exit door with his feet. His face was laced with blood, the side of his head scraped away, leaving bone and sinew. The plane was filling up fast. I crawled through three feet of water, tasting the salt, shivering. We managed to loosen the door, and

Arnie yanked at a lifeboat. Suddenly, there was a great whoosh, and we were sucked out into the vast ocean.

Instinctively kicking upwards, I prayed that the meager light above wasn't too far away. The raft thundered past me on its way to the surface and I grabbed at a rope and rode that son of a bitch all the way up until it burst through the waves and sent me flying. I swam for it and latched on like a baby to a nipple, pulling myself up in the sudden sunshine that seemed oddly out of place in the middle of my darkest day.

Nobody else broke the surface. "Arnie! Josh! Ronnie!" I shouted, but the only sound was the hungry waves lapping at the raft. Paddling back to the point of impact, I gingerly slid out and into the ocean, holding the rope by one hand, sticking my face underwater, looking for the plane. It was gone.

I swam frantically in circles, thinking it had to still be close to the surface. There was nothing when I peered into the water but a deep green staring back.

Here's the part that will take me straight to hell when I die. I gave up. Just like that. A better person might have dived under the waves to find that plane, help somebody else out. Instead, I slid back on the raft and started bawling like a baby. I drew my knees up to my chest and cried into my wet uniform like the sniveling coward that I am. Took my fist and slammed the side of my head. "Get off this raft, you asshole, and look for the guys."

Only, I didn't, because I was scared, wounded, and so damned glad to still be breathing, that I was paralyzed with indecision and basted in self-preservation.

After a few hours of paddling around, half-heartedly looking for signs of anybody, a severed arm bobbed to the surface. Repelled, I drew back, afraid to bring it on board with me. What use would that be to the poor guy now? Once again, I drew heavy mojo from the Devil, because I let it drift away. Was it Arnie? Josh? Should I have cradled that arm in my lap and given it solace and comfort? I'll never know because just like somebody flipped a switch, I passed out. When I woke, night had come, and I was gazing up at a moon that was so full, it looked like a searchlight.

---

When I was six, my father took me down to a bend in the river on the farm to teach me to swim. I was nervous that day. The water was warm and muddy near shore, but there was a current out in the middle. I clung close to the bank and Pops, my toes digging into the soft surface of the riverbed. My father held me under my arms as I spread my legs like a frog on the surface of the water, kicking frantically while holding my breath, getting nowhere.

"Milo, relax," Pops said, gently pulling me a little farther out into the channel. The water was cooler, tugging a bit at my legs, my arms.

"Don't let go," I begged, and Pops clasped me firmly to his chest. I remember the tickle of his hair, the heat from his body, the warmth of the sun. Slowly, I began to kick in cadence, dipping my face into the river, gaining some confidence. After a time, he loosened his grip a little and we slipped downstream in a dreamy state, watching the trees go by, the sky turn a bit. The current picked up its pace, swirling into a green eddy, the leaves and clouds circling above. Panicked, I reached out and grasped my father's strong arm.

"I'm right here, Milo. Let yourself go and enjoy the water." His arm was my lifeline. His voice my savior. I thought of the arm I saw from the crash, wondering if whoever lost it was a father, and began to cry.

I wanted Pops here now. He'd know what to do. Yeah, I'm a man, I guess. The Air Force thought so, even though at eighteen I was pretty wet behind the ears. Signing up for the War was the easiest decision I ever made. After all, those bastards bombed Pearl Harbor. All the guys were marching down to the recruitment office and enlisting.

We were going to beat them down, save America, rescue the rest of the world. God and Might was behind us. We flooded the airplanes, the U Boats, the sandy beaches, and far-away countries like hornets, our uniforms stiff and new, boots spit-polished, guns shining in a great migration that tilted the world on its axis.

But the sad truth is that God doesn't hand out medals, or fluff our pillows at night, nor guarantee a soft landing. War is messy. It's brimming with tears and battle cries, cannons, and the rat-a-tat of machine guns. It's filled with body parts that fly through the air like fledglings, landing in thuds on sandy beaches. Shock dealt a harsh hand as we realized this wasn't some romantic endeavor, designed to don our armor and return triumphant. This was a death card. The Ace of Spades with a bullet through the heart. And there is nothing to do, nothing to do at all, but keep moving forward because stopping isn't an option and living is a luxury.

---

The raft floats aimlessly. At first, my instinct was to paddle towards something. But what? Where? As far as I could see, there was water. The sky arcs into it like a bowl with nothing in between. Not even some lost seagull.

I don't know about ocean navigation. Nor constellations. Shit, I could hardly find North back on the farm. But I learned enough about animals to know that if no birds are flying overhead, I'm pretty far from land. Animals don't do foolish things, like sign up for a war and find themselves so far from home that they can't find their way back. They conserve energy. Use their instincts.

We heard terrible stories about sharks getting the poor guys who ended up here in the drink. The first day or so, I was petrified. Every time I saw the sun glint off a wave, I thought it was a fin coming up to buzz me. Once I pissed off the side of the raft and a fish bubbled up to the surface to investigate. I nearly shit my pants. I kept my arms and legs inside the raft, scanned the water over and over again, until exhausted. In the end, will it matter? I'm either going to starve out here, be eaten by a shark, or get shot by a Jap plane, bobbing around like a big yellow target on a cloth of blue.

There's nothing to keep me company but the sky. In the day, the sun thrashes over me like an avenging knight, peeling the skin off my body and lashing at the raft until I am baking in an oven of rubber. Watching it set each night is a celebration. I blow it a kiss, then give it the finger. "Up yours, Sun," I shout. "Send some rain, would ya?" I nestle into the darkness, turning my face to the sky, and try to remember the names of the constellations. I am at a loss after the Milky Way. I know there's a warrior up there, Orion, and I'm hoping those stars see me and come for me, not leave me like I left my fellow flyboys behind, sucking down sea water in a deathly thirst.

Sometimes I think about diving overboard and swimming until I can't swim anymore. Let my body join my buddies at the bottom of the ocean. But there's always that little flicker of hope. Maybe the Japs won't find me. Maybe my guys will. A friendly ship cutting through the water. A rope thrown to me. A shower. Meal. Paper to write back home and tell them I'm alive. Then I'm hit again with the terrible guilt of living when the others didn't. The shame of grasping for safety instead of morality like some wild thing.

———✦———

I have a girl back home. Jane. We met at a barn dance a couple of years ago. Jane's a farm girl, with blond hair like corn silk and big green eyes. Every Saturday night, I slicked down my hair, put on a fresh shirt, and drove the truck over to her place, where we sat on the porch swing and talked and laughed until the fireflies came out. Her mother poked her head out the door like a little wren popping out of a cuckoo clock, bringing us cookies and milk, remarking on the night air, fluttering her apron over the railing like she was beating a rug.

Jane cried when I enlisted. She stood on the railroad platform with Pops and Mom, waving until they were nothing but specks in the distance. We wrote to each other a few times, but once I entered the war zone, letters were scarce. I dream of her silky skin, her wide smile, the way strands of hair caught against her lips after we kissed, me brushing them away with a shaking finger. I close my eyes and knead the raft, dreaming that I am touching Jane's breasts, the curve of her hip.

I think of Jane and Mom and Pops, and squint one eye at the raft, wondering if the gold star in the window back home will be the same color.

Tonight, the sky is black. Full of thunderclouds that are sending down droplets of rain that pelt my face, feed my tongue, and shake up the ocean until I am riding it like a winged horse. It hit me hard just how much the stars mean to me now that they hide behind the night. They're a beacon of light. Thousands of eyes that peer down from the depths of the Universe.

Just one star. That's all I need to guide me. The star can tell me what to do. "Come back!" I shout at the sky, and there's not even an echo. Just the slow dirge of my heart and the groaning of the raft. My hand slides up and down on the rope, wondering if it's enough to hang myself. I rub it across my cheek, pretending its Jane's hair, and beg it to unravel and form a ladder straight up to heaven, deliver me home. Or send just one star.

# SARGE
Michael C. Keith

*I think you can honour the sacrifices of a common soldier without glorifying war. —Geraldine Brooks*

It's 1962 and I'm into my seventh month as a supply room clerk at a missile base on the coastline of the Yellow Sea in Korea when Sergeant Brennan shows up. He's my former boss's replacement and he's a lot older than I expect. We shake hands and I notice a scar running the length of his left cheek. His eyes are watery and he looks exhausted, like he hasn't slept in days.

"Good to meet you, Specialist Keith," he says, his hand damp and limp.

"Mike, Sarge," I say.

"Yeah, okay . . . Sarge is fine. Call me *Sarge*, Mike."

He drops his sagging body into the chair behind the desk he figures is his and then asks what's on tap for the day.

"About to hit the road to make my rounds," I answer.

My primary job is to drive the supply truck up to ASCOM City (military distribution center) to pick up base supplies, mostly laundry and food for the guard dogs. It takes me from around 0900 until mid-afternoon to make the run, and I do it five days a week. I'm glad to be out on the road on my own. Sitting in the supply room makes me antsy, and already I think it would be worse with this lifer in my face.

"Oh," he says, making it sound more like a question. "You drive the supply truck."

"Do it every day, Sarge."

"Good, well, I'll familiarize myself with things while you're gone and probably have lots of questions when you get back," he says, and begins to cough loudly.

When I return to the base around 1530 hours, the supply

room is empty. I look for Sarge, but the guy who runs the medic's station across the hall tells me that he's gone to his room in the NCO quarters.

"He wasn't feeling too good. Gave him some APCs," says my buddy, Corporal Rick Mosley, when I ask. "Think he's got a drinking problem. Looks like a rummy. Could smell booze on him."

---

The next morning I'm getting ready to head out and Sarge shows up looking none too steady.

"Morning," he says, going directly to the pot of coffee I just made and pouring himself a cup.

His hand shakes as he lifts the mug to his lips.

"You okay, Sarge?"

"Sure, still getting my legs back after 20 days on the Breck," he says.

"I came over on the *Breckenridge*, too," I respond enthusiastically, but he doesn't seem to hear me.

"Was supposed to fly here, but things got screwed up. Didn't feel right as soon as that ship left Oakland. Couldn't keep anything down. Same as the last time."

"Were you here during the war?" I ask.

He begins to cough again, and it causes the contents of his cup to spill on his fatigues.

"Goddamn it," he growls, wiping at his shirt and then his mouth.

There's blood on his handkerchief, and he notices that I've noticed, and he tucks it into his pocket.

"Was here when the shit was flying, son. Not such a nice place to be back then. Hell of a lot better now from the look of things. Got a little banged up when I was here the last time," he says, running his finger over his scar.

"Must have been real bad," I say and gather my things for

my day on the road.

"Wasn't good," says Sarge as I'm on my way out of the supply room. "Got pretty ugly. Stay out of the wars if you can, Mike, or you'll end up like me."

The sound of his hacking follows me halfway to the motor pool. *Poor guy*, I think, wondering how his full story must read.

---

The following week, I'm sitting at my desk and, suddenly, Sarge collapses. When I reach him, his face is already turning blue and there's foam bubbling from his lips.

"Rick," I shout. "Get in here, Sarge is in trouble."

The medic shows up in a matter of seconds and surveys the situation. By now, I'm worried that Sarge is dead.

"Christ!" he blurts. "Damned if I'll give him mouth-to-mouth," says Rick. "Be right back."

He returns in a minute with an oxygen tank and places its mask on Sarge's face. To my great relief, he comes around almost immediately. By now, the captain is in the supply room having heard the uproar from his office down the hall.

"Get the ambulance truck, Rick, and get him to the hospital."

I accompany both medic and patient to the medical facility in Seoul. On the way, Sarge is in and out of consciousness, but by the time we reach the hospital, he seems a lot better and asks us to take him back to the base.

"Can't do it. The captain ordered us to bring you here. You need to be checked over," says Rick.

"C'mon, guys. I'm fine. Just got a little dizzy is all. I'm okay, really."

Despite Sarge's claims, the attending doctor thinks otherwise, and he is checked in for tests. We return to our base, and several days pass before we're told he is being shipped back to the states for more extensive treatment. Whatever his medical problem is, we never hear.

"Don't know what the hell is going on with Brennan," says our First Sergeant when I ask for more details. "Guy's a hard drinker. Think the sauce is killing him. Too bad, he's really paid his dues. Took some hard hits during the wars."

"*Wars*, Sarge?" I ask.

"Yup, he served in World War II *and* Korea. Got a bronze star and two purple hearts. Poor bastard deserves better. Real damn hero. Think it screwed him up good. Lousy personal life. Divorce and all that shit. It's why he stayed active so long. Should have retired long ago, but no place else to go, I guess."

Later, I sit in Rick's office and we both agree that Sarge got a raw deal in life.

"Man, it's a heck of a way to end up after going through what he did," I say, adding that I hope he'll be okay.

"He seemed like a good guy. Reminded me of my uncle. He used to hit the booze pretty hard, too, after his wife died. Maybe he'll get help back home. Sad how some guys end up," remarks Rick.

———— ♦ ————

Two weeks later, the base commander catches me as I'm walking to my truck to start my day, and he tells me that Sarge died of a brain hemorrhage on his way back to the states. It was news I couldn't shake from my thoughts as I drove through the bleak winter countryside of South Korea.

Now, more than a half-century later, I can still see Sarge lying there on the supply room floor as if it all happened yesterday. The memory I have of that old soldier is still vivid. General MacArthur had it wrong; some old soldiers never fade away.

I hadn't read much back then, but something that must have come out of a book filled my head as I made my designated stops the day I was told that Sarge had died: "It's so much darker when even a dim light goes out."

# ROME 1973
Todd McKie

Marginalia and I sat side by side on a velvet sofa in her apartment above Via Arenula drinking amaretto from teacups. When she'd carried the cups into the living room, I must have looked surprised.

"Something wrong?" she asked.

"No, not at all," I said.

But it troubled me, drinking that horrible, syrupy liqueur from a teacup, instead of a proper glass. I was equally alarmed by the SS insignia on the teacups: angular, blood-red letters outlined in black.

Marginalia smiled sweetly, apologetically. "The war," she said, fluttering her free hand in the air as she sipped her amaretto.

I gulped mine and set the awful cup on the coffee table.

Six months earlier, fresh from art school, I'd moved from Philadelphia to Rome to become a great painter. Rent was cheap, food was cheap, and so was wine. The museums were cheap. Paint was cheap, canvas too. The almighty dollar was king.

I met Signorina Tazarini at a post office where I'd gone to mail a postcard to my parents, assuring them I was still fine, the weather was still fine, and, no, I hadn't been kidnapped or stabbed to death yet, and I missed them both. The photo on the postcard was of The Catacombs: hundreds of human skulls, ribcages, arm bones, finger bones, and leg bones piled in a dark basement. I'd written, "Wish you were here!" across the picture.

I was about to put a stamp on the postcard when an attractive, fashionably dressed woman of about thirty-five approached me. "Do you speak English?" she asked.

"A little," I replied.

She laughed and pointed to the stamp. "Do you want me to lick that for you?"

And now, a week later, I was in her apartment, pretending I spent all my Saturday nights with exotic, older women. Bilingual women with classic Roman noses, black hair, and deep brown eyes. I knew almost nothing about my hostess, except that she worked as a voice actor at Cinecittà, the large cluster of film studios on the outskirts of Rome, and that she'd studied American Literature at NYU. Her English was practically flawless, in vivid contrast to my sorry Italian.

"*Ti piace il jazz?*" asked Marginalia.

"*Che cosa?*" I managed.

"Jazz music, silly. Do you like it?"

I didn't like jazz, but what could I say? Our relationship was just beginning and I didn't want it to come to an abrupt halt before we got to know each other more intimately. Honesty is always the best policy, I reasoned, but perhaps its implementation could be delayed for a while.

"I love jazz," I confessed.

"Well, then, jazz will be the soundtrack *della nostra storia d'amore.*" Marginalia winked at me, and then, a moment later, snorted.

She had a cruel streak, I realized, and that knowledge turned what had been a slight stirring in my trousers into an actual boner. Instinctively, I rested a hand in my lap, hoping to conceal my mischievous member.

Marginalia wasn't fooled. "Ah," she said softly, "a tree grows in Brooklyn."

Just then, a thunderous clatter arose from the street below. Marginalia ran to the window.

"Cavalli!" she screamed. "Hundreds of horses. Come look!"

By the time I reached the window, the last few horses were

disappearing around the corner onto Largo Argentina. The sound of hooves became fainter and fainter still and then was gone. In its wake, the rich smell of horse manure filled the air.

Turning from the window, Marginalia took my hand in hers. "So many horses," she murmured, "so little time."

Her bedroom was spare and, except for a framed poster of Mussolini waving from a balcony, free of decoration. A record player and a few albums sat atop a white enamel table. Marginalia slipped a record from its sleeve and placed it on the turntable. A terrible honking and squealing commenced. Jazz clarinet music! My least favorite of all the musical idioms in the entire goddamn universe.

"Acker Bilk!" hollered Marginalia. "Dig it, *mein kleine putzen katze*!"

Those hideous teacups, and now she was speaking German! Maybe, I thought, I should get out of there while I could.

Marginalia, though, was transformed by the music. She leapt onto the bed. In seconds, she'd removed her shoes, scarf, blouse, and skirt. She hopped back and forth on the bed in her underwear. The brassiere was standard-issue stuff, but Marginalia's silken panties were patterned with images of equine paraphernalia: saddles, horseshoes, bridles, bits, and halters. Prancing and twirling to the jazzy clarinet, she cried, "Tally ho!" and, "*Avanti, cavalli*!"

I wondered where I fit into the action, if it all. Was I to be participant or spectator? Marginalia danced as if possessed, her frenzy reminding me of whirling dervishes I'd seen in National Geographic. Those Sufi spinners were said to carry sabers beneath their robes. I felt relieved that Marginalia had nothing to hide in that department, until she reached beneath her pillow and extracted a riding crop. She shook it and swatted me playfully. Then she began whacking me in earnest, shrieking, "Giddyup, Roy Rogers!"

Suddenly, we heard, above the music, an insistent pounding

at the door and a deep, booming, "Gina! Gina! *Apri la porta!*"

Marginalia stood still. She cocked her head. She jumped from the bed and raked the needle from the record.

"Who is it?" I whispered as Marginalia dressed hastily.

"It's my brother, Carlo," she said. "Jump out the window!"

The pounding at the door became fiercer. Marginalia threw open the window and pushed me toward it. "Out!" she commanded.

I hesitated. Her apartment was on the fourth floor.

A deafening crash, the sound of wood splintering. A moment later, a huge, swarthy man rushed into the bedroom holding an ax above his head.

I leapt from the window. While plummeting to certain death, I reviewed my life: a few highlights here and there, but, generally speaking, a slideshow of regret.

Instead of landing on the pavement with every bone in my body crushed, my skull split open and me dead, I fell onto the awning of the trattoria on the ground floor and bounced from it onto a display case full of seafood. I lay sprawled among the crushed ice, the calamari, swordfish steaks, mussels, lemon wedges, clams, and a spiny lobster.

The few couples dining al fresco stared at me, briefly, then turned away, whispering to one another, glancing furtively in my direction again, and, their curiosity satisfied, returned to their spaghetti vongole, their fritto misto di mare, their bottles of cool Frascati.

From my icy vantage point, I could see the windows of Marginalia's apartment. Nothing moved within, but did I see, backlit, a silhouette of a couple embracing? Probably a coincidence of shadows, lighting, perspective. Then, in case Carlo and his ax were hot-footing it downstairs, I decided it might be best to move on.

I hopped from the display case, brushing ice and seafood from my jacket, and strolled away, sending a message, I hoped, that this sort of thing happened all the time and was merely another facet of my dashing lifestyle. The bracing scent of horseshit lingered in the air as, peeking nervously over my shoulder, I walked toward Campo de' Fiori.

A tall, thin fellow juggled cats in the center of the plaza. He'd attracted a large crowd. The cats, of all shapes and sizes, didn't seem to mind being juggled. I stood at the back of the crowd, marveling at the juggler's skill, the eerie composure of the cats. I watched until the performance ended, then dropped a hundred lira note in the juggler's basket.

Delighted by my generosity, I ambled away. I'd helped a fellow artist, and although his medium was kinetic sculpture, and mine the traditional one of oil paint on canvas, weren't we brothers in art? In truth, weren't all of us earthlings—chimps, homo sapiens, brainy dolphins, elephants, songbirds, squid, bugs, and amoebic slime—brothers and sisters?

Fueled by this noble sentiment, my thoughts were those of a madman. I slapped myself hard in the face. My jolly mood darkened somewhat and I felt like myself again.

I walked to the river, across Ponte Garibaldi and into Trastevere, where I lived in a grim attic that doubled as my studio. I had a sickly-sweet taste in my mouth from the amaretto and an idea for a painting in my head: a dark cobalt sky, an ancient palazzo, a giant with an ax, a beatnik horse playing a clarinet and, raining down on all of it, hundreds of cats.

Cutting down an alley behind the Basilica of Our Lady of Eternal Sorrow, whose interior displayed Saint Cecilia's nose in an ornate vitrine, I heard footsteps behind me. Wouldn't it be awful—and tragically ironic—if I were hacked to pieces before I reached the shelter of my attic and began work on my masterpiece? I quickened my pace.

# CHARIOT
Tamra Plotnick

Love is a chariot
of the mind,
galloping to distant territories
where you don't know
the language
nor the customs.

The language of relationships,
    treaties, diplomacy,
will be called for later…perhaps,
and may require translators,
guidebooks, or ethnographies.

# LA TOMATINA
Robert Mangeot

No one knew how La Tomatina began, Elliott lectured me on cue. Already my husband brandished his archeology doctorate and tenure. Add a glass of Rioja and, apparently, he became supreme arbiter of fact and fiction. Well, we pretty little biostatisticians could read, too. I understood in my soul why one August a Spanish mob first pelted each other with crushed tomatoes. A protest, same reason they'd turned the pelting into an annual free-for-all, one precious hour a year to coat what vexed you in tomato paste.

Years ago, this was even before we had our Gabriela, Elliott and I happened on the Tomatina during one of his summer digs. I'd believed the whole idea of a mass tomato fight was nonsense—until Elliott made me try it and my stray tomato connected on his jutted chin. Every August since we had returned, faithfully. And every August since, somewhere between Chapel Hill and Buñol, Elliott broke out his same tired spiel about the Tomatina's obscure origins. This year he chose the Renfe train in from Valencia.

"A feast for the Virgin Mary, perhaps," Elliott supposed. Again. He'd also brought along a perfectly awful gaucho hat that made him look like an overripe Zorro. "Gotten mightily out of hand," Elliott said, between the dots and dashes to his Morse Code giggle. "Franco was so confounded that he banned it. Did I mention that?"

Twice this year alone. A gaze out at the sierras and olive groves hid my evil smile. Tomorrow, I'd plop a fat tomato square on Elliott's kisser, and he would plop one on mine, with a gusto that shattered his academic's cool.

At Buñol, the taxi ride should've been a short hop to our little four-star off the Plaza del Pueblo, but the trainloads and coach tours gathering clogged the narrow streets. Grungesters in their thousands drank beer and primed themselves for the metric-ton food fight ahead.

In the hotel lobby, Javier greeted us with his usual warmth and, of course, his Tio Pepe. "Señora!" he said. "You are ready to make the grand combat?"

Ready? I'd been target practicing behind the garage since March. "Viva La Tomatina!"

"*Sí, sí*! Many people this year. Much sunshine."

"Monica, darling," Elliott said, "we're getting rather old for the mosh pit. Let's just watch tomorrow, shall we?"

"Watch?" I said, and too on the rise of suspect motives. Once a year we mosh-pitted, and when the hour ended, he and I would stumble red-splattered and sticky to the four-star and make ferocious love 'til long past dark. Our aftershocks spiced up the bedroom for weeks. The same method polished our marriage as washed grit from Buñol's paving stones: tomato acid bath.

I said, "But we've bought the tickets."

"You're being silly. We'll give them away and head on to Barcelona after lunch."

"Tell him," I said to Javier. "Tell him he'll regret missing out."

Javier shrugged. "I never go near it. So crowded and such mess."

Traitor. Damned traitors, both of them.

———— ✦ ————

"I can't believe you're giving up on the Tomatina," I said over tapas, not sparing Elliott any drama either. Accusations might be all I would get to hurl. "Aren't you always saying how delightfully mysterious the festival is? How it does wonders for my skin?"

"Go alone if it matters that much to you."

"Alone? But we share the Tomatina."

Elliott rolled his eyes. He actually rolled his eyes. "Don't sulk, dear. Can't I once enjoy Spain without rinsing dried gunk from my sinuses?"

Sulking ate at him, did it? I sulked through the lamb and potatoes and on through the cod. Tempranillo and Spanish guitar roiled my pent-up grudges. Elliott had that tomato coming, one lousy tomato to purge his coffee pot hogging and toilet seat neglect and clockwork droning-on. Without Tomatina therapy, I might devolve into chucking crab cakes at his endless university parties.

Eventually, he stopped banging on about this or that local myth he'd banged on about already. "Fine," he said, "since you're going to be this way. We'll go tomorrow. If. *If if if* you promise this is our last Tomatina."

"Absolutely," I lied.

---

To battle, I wore a doomed cotton blouse and army surplus boots specially picked for wet-weather traction. Elliott chose a bull runner's outfit and scarf, not the Day-Glo orange I'd sworn made him the most dashing man in Spain. In white, he could've slipped *olé* into the Plaza jumble, except astronauts in orbit probably cracked up spotting his ridiculous Zorro hat. That monster was worth whatever small fortune he'd spent on it.

I herded Elliott into the Plaza early and staked out a spot where tomato trucks would dump fresh ammo reliably. All morning, grungesters filled in around us while I listened to him carp about our hurried breakfast, about the heat and loud music, about the festival crush, and every child there who surely, surely must be a world-class pickpocket. Let the buggers pick away—for La Tomatina I never brought anything more valuable than pride and prescription goggles.

By eleven, the crowd had swelled to cattle pen close-quarters that bulged out every crooked lane. Tradition went the first tomatoes weren't thrown until someone fetched the Serrano ham from atop a soaped pole. Grungester after grungester failed to shimmy high enough before skidding down to the paving stones. I was near abandoning post and snatching that ham myself, but finally, a girl on break from any pickpocketing climbed that pole with the ease of a lemur. A cannon boomed, and the melee began.

Success luring Elliott into so many repeat pastings was simple strategy: each year's tomato had to come on a delay and seemingly on accident. Blab about my protest theories, about my target practice, and how I found us sexual renewal, and he would analyze it to its grave. He wouldn't set foot in Buñol again. No, only when the stucco ran red and we'd each given and taken serious hits could I stealth-bomb Elliott.

Such as now. I shoved myself a bit of elbow room and crouched beneath the whizz of tomatoes. Elliott stood an easy throw away, cackling and peppering handfuls scattershot. I squished a particularly large bastard, felt its flesh and juice run through my fingers. Felt my blood boil, felt every don't-be-silly and watch-your-LDLs seep into that wad of fruit. I drew dead bead and let fly.

And missed.

Somehow, I missed. The tomato flew wide and caught a Scandinavian grungester in his chest. He and his crew returned vigorous fire—*whap whap whap*—and when I'd scraped my goggles clean, and spat pulp from my mouth, Elliott had fallen lost into the Plaza.

My hour was half-gone. Around me, grungesters and locals and pickpocket children slithered pinkish together. If life had any justice, Elliott's hat would still loom atop his head even as ruined ball caps and tee shirts sloughed off to the gutter. Justice, though, had joined my list of traitors. No Elliott, no moment of release, no telling what heap of festering grievances my life would become.

I did the unthinkable. What no sober, drunk, or stoned mind dared at the Tomatina. I clambered up a Plaza gate and, there in plain view; I shouted Elliott's name until my throat went raw. They battered me, those grungesters. Tomato after tomato after tomato, long range, and point blank.

A Zorro hat! Stained in pink camouflage and flopping woundedly, Elliott and his stupid, wonderful hat were only meters away. He and the Scandinavians slipped over themselves to shower tomatoes anywhere at anybody. Laughing, laughing, everyone laughing like freed souls, and despite the shouts and horns, I heard that giggle of Elliott's loudest of all.

I froze, my tomato locked and loaded. How did this need in me begin? How did any myth ever start, the Tomatina, the insides of a marriage, me rooting army surplus shoes firmly in Day-Glo childishness? Look at us now: graying hair, statins for cholesterol, grandparents, if our Gabriela's fertility treatments ever took. Maybe I protested not Elliot but Father Time. Father Time tapping his watch and sending me into shudders over how many more Augusts Elliott and I had left.

Elliott grinned like a schoolboy and zipped a tomato that splattered my blouse from collar to tails. God help me, I loved that man, and that was why I had no choice at all but to launch right back at him.

Someone bumped me as I let loose. Still, I thought on my crash landing, my aim had felt true. Later, at the hotel, Elliott would top off our cava, and I would tickle him and ask so-casually if today any expert tomato had hit home. While in the glow, I would plant my seeds about returning next year. However, this thing had gotten started, La Tomatina was how we stayed shiny and young.

# ANGIE'S WEDDING
Charles Joseph Albert

I was living in Austin, Texas, when I got the invitation to my sister's wedding in the southeastern part of France known as Provence. It was going to be preceded by a weeklong celebration, hosted by her future in-laws. This invitation caused a dilemma for me. For one thing, I've always bought into the French propaganda that they're the most sophisticated people in the world, and that anything French is automatically glamorous. Look at their *haute cuisine* (French for "cooking with oats"); anyone who can turn snails into *escargots à la bourguignonne* has got a handle on class.

Texas, on the other hand, was never known for sophistication. I mean, you're considered sophisticated in Texas if your pickup has a bed guard. So, for me, the big question in going to this wedding was, do I try to up my sophistication, or do I stay true to my roots and go with what I know?

On the advice of my friends and barber, I decided to wear the Texan badge proudly, as it was less likely to make me look like an ass. Besides, it would be downright unpatriotic to try to be like the French. After all, trying to look French when you're a tourist is silly. I mean, imagine you've got the beret, you've got the *baguette* ("small bag" in French), you've got the bicycle... but you're on the Eiffel Tower. Come on! Who do you think you're fooling? Any Frenchman who sees you will say, "Why ees zat teepical frenshman on zee beegest tourist trap on zee planette?!"

But, and perhaps most importantly, if I went looking like a loud, irritating Texan, I would embarrass the hell out of my Francophile sister!

After all, it was hardly fair. She was marrying this good-looking French guy, a kickboxer whose parents own a vineyard. I mean, give me a break! The only way he could have been more Harlequin Romance is if he was descended from royalty.

> He held me manfully in his bulging boxer arms. Caressing my thigh with a bottle of wine from his parent's ancient vineyard, he murmured, "Alas! The Du Tucan family fortune will be lost unless I marry an American girl, *mon amour*."
>
> "But, Raoul! *I* am American," I moaned in perfect French...

I figured the least I could do to keep her grounded was show her in-laws what a tasteless family she really came from.

As it turned out, I couldn't really bring myself to drink so much I'd embarrass my poor sister. Oh, I drank plenty. But her threshold for embarrassment was a lot higher than I counted on.

Fortunately, it wasn't only up to me to embarrass her; the rest of our family was also there. When we get together, we're enough to embarrass Larry Flint, let alone an already insecure *américain* marrying into a bunch of hoity-toity Frenchies.

But in spite of my malevolent intentions, my black Stetson and snakeskin boots were only of minor interest to them. As several wedding guests patiently explained to me, the "distinctly American" cowboy outfit is actually descended from clothes pretty common to southern France and Northern Spain, where livestock is raised.

For days before the wedding, the in-laws invited all the family and guests to a simple lunch: foie gras, truffled omelets, and twenty-year-old wines. A meal like that would cost hundreds in the US, but for them, it was almost free: they made their own foie gras, grew their own truffles, and cellared their own wine. There was no pretentiousness, no attitude, just really amazing food and *joie de vivre* ("jaw of fever" in French).

They made up for it at night with the *apéritif* ("apparent tiff," since that's when most fights break out). That's a lot like a cocktail party except that you can't skip dinner and hog down on the snacks because the snacks are wretched. There's maybe some kind of fried critter intestine on a dry cracker, itty-bitty pickles that taste like salty vinegar, and then some other insubstantial fare like candy-covered sunflower seeds. That stuff is just not a meal substitute. Plus, instead of a nice scotch for a drink, you get either a licorice-flavored alcohol called *pastis* or the evil brew known as *suze* that they make from a bitter weed unknown to you Americans, and don't look to me to ruin a good thing and tell you, it tastes like expired aspirin.

These unpleasant alcohols had the one advantage that they were 90-proof, so after a few slugs (coincidentally, also an appetizer) you really don't care what the alcohol's flavor is. I went to bed drunk and hungry.

At last, the day of the wedding came. Nowadays, the French hold the church ceremony after the required civil ceremony. So, the entire wedding party paraded first into the cramped little office of the Mayor of Cucuron, who signed the official documents. To an American, it seems strange to visit the local bureaucracy as part of the festivities, but I was told that this part of the ceremony was required by the mayor. After all, it ensured he got invited to the reception.

We guests then wound our way through the picturesque narrow streets until we made it to the humble little Catholic church on the other end of town. I was at first impressed that they didn't do a motorcade, the way Texan weddings do (preferably in Cadillac convertibles), until I realized that anything wider than a Smart car would have gotten jammed in those narrow winding streets. Also, the other end of town was only about fifteen houses away.

It was a nice walk and a good chance for me to converse with some of the local townspeople. With my masterful command of French, I was able to suavely ask a beautiful local girl, "*Voulez-vous cochon avec moi ce soir?*" (Do you want pig with me tonight?), which didn't get me very far, either with the girl or with an upgrade to my cocktail snacks.

The church itself dated from the fourteenth century, with an impressive medieval stone façade, complete with saints and gargoyles. The interior was breathtaking in its "guiltwork" (not a misspelling; remember, it's a Catholic church) and faux marble, stunningly illuminated by hundreds of cameras held by relatives. If that church were in the U.S., it would be about the most famous landmark on the continent. But tucked away in that little village, it's just another old church.

After both the civil and church ceremonies, the entire party left of one stomach for the reception. I myself was salivating the whole way back to the feast. The previous night had left me rather peckish, and I'd heard about the lavishness of French banquets.

The Main Hall of Cucuron is really the only large public space in the town; both wedding receptions per year take place there, and a springtime tractor auction, too, I think. It was new, expensive, and pretty large for a town of five hundred people. I was told that it was built by some socialist up for re-election in a little political tradition of enticements called "*le porc-baril*" (sorry, I don't know the translation).

When we got to the hall, we mingled around for a while, drinking licorice wine or weed gin. As I did not find any other French women to ask to have pig with, I was seated at one of the big long tables without incident.

And was this a banquet! Man, what a meal. I love the way the French bring it out, one dish at a time. Unlike here in the U.S., where we cram everything onto one plate so that you have to scrape salad dressing off of your pie. The French bring in course after course, and it's not just for show; it's based on medical research. It turns out that getting food served in separate dishes makes it easier for the health-conscious diner to get a new wine with each course.

First, we had a nice light red wine and some appetizers; duck liver pâté, I think. I didn't dare ask what part of the duck they make the pâté out of. Next, they brought out some *crudités* ("uncouth vegetables") with a crisp white, followed by a sautéed scallop appetizer. Then came the main course, which was mutton with a lovely rich red wine to go with it. I believe it was a *Côtes du Rhône*, but the bottle count was already getting high, so I can't substantiate that. The photographic record I have of the evening was taken much later and shows me sitting in a slightly tilted position with three empty bottles on the table in front of me.

I do remember that they brought out the salad next, after the main course, which is how they do it in France, and it makes sense because you don't have to worry about the salad cooling off while you eat everything else first.

Last, of course, came the deserts. I had heard that there was to be some fancy pastry for the meal, and I do have an evil sweet tooth, especially for chocolate. But I almost cried out in dismay when the waitperson brought only one tiny plate to the table. Okay, they looked exquisite—but they were so damn small! Was this, I wondered, why French people were all so thin? To make matters worse, there was only one chocolate item on the whole plate.

Sweat trickling down my brow, fingers tightening around the handle of my fork, I racked my brains for a polite way to warn my neighbors that I was going after the chocolate one, in case they valued their fingers.

Then, a miracle happened. The Miracle of Angie's Wedding. Aleluias and angels wafted down from the sky.

The waiter put an identical plate in front of the person next to me, and then another in front of the next person. Yes, that first platter of tiny desserts in front of me was just for me.

Tears of joy rolling down my cheek, I watched the waiter deliver his platters to the rest of the table. I was going to be able to savor every one of those beautiful little desserts myself. Once again, I had a *raison d'être* ("raisin debt").

This curious experience of homicidal greed, and subsequent rush of guilty joy, stuck in my mind, and I talked to my brothers about it afterward. It turned out that they had exactly the same thoughts as I, even down to securing a knife as an arguing point for the éclair.

I'm not sure, but I think the moral here is that Americans are overexposed to violence.

Anyway, the burden of ingesting all that sugar sobered me up enough to observe the serving of the champagne, which was pretty cool, because they poured it down a pyramid of glasses, the flow filling each glass in the stack in sequence. This mirrored the serving of the traditional French wedding *croque-en-bouche* (French for "frog in a bush"), which is a huge pile of puff pastry stuck together in a pyramid with hardened syrup. It's what the French serve instead of a wedding cake.

We spent a while thinking up lame drunken toasts, which we found uproariously funny since we were, after all, drunk. Then came the dancing.

The French are funny about their dancing. They don't just go out dancing for a few hours. If you're going to go, you go all night. Also, they don't have any good music of their own, so they use old American disco music.

So, we danced cheesy disco dances and drank until we were falling down. Then at around 5 a.m., two of the groom's so-called friends came and got my younger brother and me and we went off to short sheet the matrimonial bed and other kinds of charming jokes, before going back and collapsing in our own beds.

The next afternoon, we managed to crawl out of bed and re-congregate at the same hall for lunch. We each looked like hundred-pound grape barrels had landed on our heads, which is actually not far from what really happened.

I learned a charming new expression for people who let their future brothers-in-law get them drunk: *gueule de bois* ("gullible").

As we straggled in to finish off the leftovers, the new in-laws told corny jokes and sang silly songs. We hung out all afternoon, eating leftovers at the community center, sipping the local wine, looking out on the ancient stone architecture of the village with its beautiful broad-leafed plane trees reaching over the village square, and as I looked at the friendly, ruddy faces around the room, I began to understand for the first time that my sister wasn't going to come home. Why should she? How could her quality of life possibly be better anywhere but here? And I realized that for all our sibling rivalries and antagonism, I was going to miss her terribly.

I set down my wine glass and tried to hide the terrific whirlpool of self-pity I was sinking into. I think I succeeded, because no one burst into "Milord," that campy Edith Piaf song where she cheers up a jilted Englishman. The mere thought of it eventually made me smile through my tears. And then and there I vowed to come back every year to see her and her husband. In fact, I am writing this from their guest bedroom now. It's a hardship, I admit, but no sacrifice is too great for my sister's sake.

Now, if you'll excuse me, I hear the dinner bell…

# R.O.T. RALLIES
Jill Hawkins

We return like perennials
to Austin rallying with
lawyers and strippers on
Harleys and substance
in this heat of 6th street
bartenders built to win sashes
mix our whiskey drinks
knowing tomorrow it will
be Shiner Bock in Luckenbach
sweating out an old tune
familiar and favored
with old friends and new
acceptance is swung by
right leg over a motor
it's legitimate in leather
breast wars, like heat strokes
it only happens in season

# BITE ME
Jeanine Pfeiffer

The word is pronounced rrrrrrANGG-ohng. A brief vocal overture with the tongue playing timpani and horn. Emphasis on the first syllable, rolling the r's, nestling the tongue back against the roof of the mouth for the "ng" sounds.

For the uninitiated, a bit of tongue play is needed before the word rolls out nicely. To achieve full effect, ranggong should be forcefully expelled while leaping backwards in terror. This is the typical enunciation in the shocked pause following a ranggong encounter.

I learned the Manggarai word for scorpions the morning I forewent my pseudo-Buddhist convictions and smacked one into mush. In the tropics, we grow accustomed to being surprised by stinging whatsits: that is how they introduce themselves. They sting first and we ask questions later, such as: "Ouch! What the *&%bleep*&% was that?!"

Prickly fruits and forest vines, stinging bushes and nettles, ants, flies, hornets, beetles, mosquitoes, scorpions, scorpion fish, catfish, jellyfish, lionfish, rays, cone shells, and anemones. Manggarai whip dances and dishes containing scalding doses of chili pepper. They all sting.

Indonesia, a 17,500-island megadiversity hotspot, hosts a plethora of scorpions and scorpion-like creatures, including a giant midnight-blue forest scorpion packing lobster claws. Indonesia being Indonesia, new species are constantly being discovered: an eyeless forest litter scorpion in Maluku, a tailless whip scorpion on Borneo[1]. Or the "water scorpion" of Flores Island: a seductive taxonomic mystery whose pincer-like arms resemble a true scorpion's.

Fortunately, the water scorpion, also known as the "water boatman," is, in truth, a bug. A beefy, thumb-sized bug who breathes through a built-in snorkel in its tail or, more charmingly, by embracing an underwater air bubble. The Tado, my adoptive Manggarai clan whose name refers to both people and place, have bestowed a grandiose name on their native water scorpion: *empo wae* — "Grandfather of the Water."

Like most critters with biting, pinching, or stinging parts, my first water scorpion had impeccable timing. It found me half-naked. Our introduction occurred on the Racang river, the only waterway on Tado lands gushing deliciously along its entire length, even during the dry season. Ordinarily, river bathing is a treat. Far better than public bathing at the village water pump or beneath a trickling bamboo tube, where all ablutions take place beneath the cover of a large cloth sarong, such that nothing more scandalous than a shoulder or an ankle is revealed to curious onlookers.

I try my utmost to adhere to traditional bathing codes, yet the contortions required while encased in a skin-tight sarong leave me only partially soaped or rinsed, weary of constantly re-cinching the knot decorously secured across my breastbone. Bathing in rivers allows for equally modest, yet less strenuous gymnastics: dipping my entire body into masses of flowing water is much easier than trying to direct rivulets down an armpit or more inaccessible parts.

So there I was, standing in the river trying to get clean, or in the words of my long-departed (human) Grandma, "washing up as far as possible, washing down as far as possible, and then washing possible." A rather delicate setting, with so much exposed skin. I was focusing on body parts, not so much on my watery surroundings — a forgivable lapse for a bather untrained in aquatic entomology.

Not that it mattered. Instead of manifesting in its usual form, a dullish black exoskeleton easily camouflaged in darkened waters, Grandfather zinged past my ear with his flying apparatus extended, revealing lurid folds of red, blue, and black. I inhaled sharply: this was a miniature invertebrate superhero, an animated character from a blockbuster movie suddenly gone 3-D and bursting off screen.

At the time, standing dumbstruck in the water, I had no idea of what the creature was. Hummingbirds don't exist in Indonesia. Sunbirds, their evolutionary counterpart, do, but the colors I saw didn't correlate with sunbird hues. The next possibility, a rhinoceros beetle — also large, black, with massive pincers and buzzing when flying — came to mind, but samples collected by our community-based research team never deviated from a monochromatic scheme. Plus, the rhinoceros beetles' favored habitat centered around coconut palms in household gardens, not scruffy riverside vegetation.

Hmmmmm.

I was vaguely familiar with the faded-black version of the water scorpion, as we had several specimens, their wings and appendages folded into inert carapaces floating in bottles of diluted alcohol in the Tado Community Research Center. But the zooming, outrageously colored thing that just whipped past my shoulder? That was new.

It wasn't until I described my encounter to Kanisius, a research associate responsible for our insectarium, that we made the connection between dead specimen and living specimen, and the water scorpion became my new favorite insect[2].

Grandfathers of the Water are amphibious, aerodynamic, and musically inclined. Species of water boatman in Europe have distinguished themselves as the world's loudest animal, an achievement potentially nonsensical until we do the calculations. Water boatmen produce the loudest sound relative to body size: 99.2 decibels, similar to a passing freight train. Sadly, only submerged creatures with excellent eyesight can fully appreciate the boatman's stridulations: sounds produced by rubbing a penis the width of a hair across corrugations on his abdomen. (Could any creature, no matter how segmented their thorax is, perform a more brilliant seduction?)

Outside of the concert arena, empo wae are carnivorous ambush predators, hunting tiny freshwater shrimp, fish, tadpoles, and mosquito larvae. They kill with a one-two punch: an immobilizing sting followed by an injection of digestive enzymes, allowing the victim's tissues to be sucked up like slimy spaghetti. (Not that my sixty-kilogram, dripping wet self could be reduced to limp pasta by a bug the size of my toe. Or, at least not this particular bug.)

Back to scorpion-scorpions. The western Indonesian version of the house scorpion, known as kalacengkeng (kahl-ah-JENG-kehng: a lyrical, playful-sounding word meaning "scorpion with its butt in the air"), are espresso-black and feisty.

I have seen hundreds of these feisty-butted scorpions. Strolling through a crowded roadside market in south Jakarta in the mid-1990s, I observed, in fascinated horror, the direct-marketing strategies of a Javanese herbal medicine (obat) salesman. Short, stocky, bearded, and wild-eyed, he promoted scorpion bite remedies from a stool centered in a light blue plastic basin. A hand-lettered sign purveyed his wares: "Obat Kalacenkeng, Rupiah 1500."

The sign was overkill, because swarms of scorpions merrily bustled over every visible millimeter of his body. The man was a living Hitchcockian moment, erupting with scorpions, while he smiled, apparently unperturbed, and gesticulated while shouting out the merits of his wares over the heads of nonplussed passersby, his singsong advertorial a running commentary on the amazing properties of his scorpion-bite medicine.

An ethnoecologist by training — and thus duty-bound to honor species' multiple roles in both cultures and ecosystems — I remain ambivalent toward creepy crawlies. Scorpions have earned permanent status on the list of Top Ten Critters Who

Make Me Shudder. Yet, I appreciate their insouciant nature, their structural elegance, and the immediate potency of their toxins.

In Manggarai villages, we are on perpetual scorpion alert, and everyone has a bite story, the Indonesian equivalent of cockroach encounters. Scorpions and cockroaches may belong to different entomological orders, but as residents of the southeastern United States can attest, there are scary, buzzing roaches that bite: ask anyone who's had a close encounter of the bizarre kind with a recently disturbed palmetto bug, frenetically zoom-smacking its way into one's airspace.

I have my own unforgettable palmetto bug story: eight years old in Florida, opening a cousin's infested dollhouse that languished in storage for far too long, my delight and anticipation napalmed into running-away-screaming horror as the denizens sprouted six legs and winged carapaces, and an equally memorable scorpion story.

Mid-afternoon on a weekend in Tado, I was finishing work in the Tado Community Research Center before heading over to a village social event. I expected one of the usual rather desultory rural gatherings involving coffee, cigarettes, and overly sweet desserts to celebrate the anniversary of a death, or a first communion, or a child's completion of middle school, or some other reason to flaunt the host's financial ability to throw a party. I wasn't looking forward to the requisite bland chitchat, but the promise of imported baked goods (a rarity) titillated my taste buds.

I wrapped up my work, grabbed my travel bag, and snapped the leash onto my long-haired Chihuahua, Muku. Traversing the office, I made it midway across the floor when a sudden stabbing pain shot through my big toe. I shrieked and scooped up Muku in the same instant.

No need to look down to confirm the culprit. Once you've been inducted, the signature pain of a scorpion sting is easily identifiable, whether the perpetrator is strikingly obvious or quasi-invisible. I was in perfect scorpion habitat: our Center was roofed with thatch, walled with bamboo, and floored with cement. Unlike their shiny black cousins in the western half of the archipelago, eastern Indonesian scorpions are perfectly color-coordinated to match human settings. Cryptically grayish or translucently tan, Flores scorpions scuttle everywhere humans are, blending in with dirt, bamboo, wood, concrete, and the occasional peeling linoleum. The ultimate stealth-stingers, abetted by the Asian custom of no shoes indoors.

Swearing and stumbling, I hobbled to the doorway and crumpled on the concrete sill, gripping my bitten foot in one hand, my dog in the other. Staring out at the hillside scenery — nobody within sight — I resigned myself to being stuck. This was the era before reliable motorcycle taxi service, and the few public minivans sporadically plying the roadways could take hours to appear, if they did at all.

The road wasn't within hollering distance, anyhow. No way to call for help. No landlines, cell phones, pagers, satellite units, or walkie-talkies. There wasn't even a gosh-darn tin can rigged up to a clothesline. I could limp to the local posyandu (public clinics staffed by someone with a health diploma), but their schedule was erratic, the clinic rarely open. Their few boxes of government-supplied medication ran out during the first week of every month, leaving the community to fend for itself or travel long distances to the more distant puskesmas (larger clinics with basic laboratory facilities and more staff), even if all a person needed was aspirin.

A scorpion-bite neophyte (this was only my second sting), I had no idea of what to do. Lance it like a boil? Apply pressure? Suck the poison out? Ice would be nice, but there was no chance of procuring it within the vicinity: the nearest refrigerator was twenty kilometers away.

I resorted to Plan E: gazing out the doorway and gritting my teeth. The Center sat squarely along a water buffalo-herding path and was an object of curiosity. Folks made it their business to routinely check in; I knew someone would show up eventually.

Sure enough, several agonizing pain cycles later, one of my uncles from the 'hood hiked up the hillside carrying a bundle of grass thatch panels, on his way to a roof repair.

"*Selamat* — good afternoon," Uncle greeted me. "*Gimana* — what's up?"

"Scorpion bite," I squeezed out through clenched molars. Involuntary tears stung my eyes. "*Ada musa* — is there any sort of medicine available?" I asked, deliberately using the Manggarai word for traditional herbal remedies, because I sensed no store-bought pharmaceuticals would provide relief.

"I'll be right back," he replied, dropping the panels to the ground and hopping nimbly over a ridge to climb into the lower branches of a Ceylon oak[3] tree. I watched him pull a few leaves off, stuff them into his mouth, and then leap back to the ground.

"Can you stretch out your leg?" he asked. "Show me where you were bit."

I did, and after chewing the leaves and spitting them into his hand, uncle gently applied a poultice of masticated goo around my toe, assuring me the pain would subside. Rubbing more globs around my foot, he added extra spit and a prayer with his callused hand on my knee for good measure.

Then he sat down and, with a chuckle, entertained me with detailed family remedies for various types of common bites — snake, rat, wasp, bee, centipede. Scorpion, no big deal. Plenty of other bitey critters to contend with, and did I tell you about the time I climbed up a tree to trim some branches, was surprised by a green mamba, hacked its head off with my machete and killed the snake, but still got bit when I stepped on the dead mamba's open jaws because I wasn't looking where I put my foot on my way down? Adu, did my leg swell up! It was unrecognizable!

The poultice helped, the stories helped, and the immediate, authentic caring from my uncle helped even more. Yet my foot still ached. Badly. Mustering reserves of social-grace-under-pressure, I smoothed my face into a smile and nodded along as he chatted.

It wasn't easy. The after-bite was intense. Unrelenting stabs pulsed beneath my skin, at times leaving me gasping. Dagger-wielding demons inside my foot mounted a vigorous jabbing contest where no side was winning, so each side dug in and redoubled their efforts. The toxins seared and throbbed in different directions every few minutes. The pain didn't go away in any reasonable sense of time. It took hours.

Of course, such an incident was incredibly newsworthy. Foreign Scientist Bit by Scorpion and She's Down for the Count, buzzed along the community grapevine, spreading the word up and down the highway. In record time, the village head showed up, followed by the Tado chief and several elders, all abandoning the party to come check on me.

"*Kenapa* — what happened?" asked each visitor as they stepped through the Center's door. Aware that everyone knew perfectly well what had happened (otherwise they wouldn't have shown up to witness the aftermath), I retorted, "*diinjak oleh gajah* — an elephant stomped on my foot," and was rewarded with chuckles.

Woven mats were hauled out and spread across the cement floor, extending our seating area. I handed a fistful of crumpled rupiah bills to a youngster to go buy bottles of soda pop and crackers. Halfway through recounting more venomous tales, we found another scorpion, dead and being picked over by ants, next to the mat I was sitting on. Everyone recoiled for a nanosecond, then an uncle picked up the corpse and flung it out the door.

"One day I was taking down a towel from the wash line and there was a scorpion hidden inside. It bit me on the hand. Those bites can last for quite a while," an auntie sympathized.

"If you swept your floor more frequently, you wouldn't have as many problems with scorpions," another auntie recommended, sniffing pointedly around the dusty Center.

"A scorpion bite on the nose of a water buffalo can kill it," an uncle asserted.

"Most adults can handle two, three, five bites — no problem," countered the chief.

Once we ran out of enticing conversation topics, the elders realized they were missing out on party goodies (the chief was a sucker for free cups of coffee and sugary treats), so they took their leave, promising to send back someone with a motorcycle to haul me home.

This time, I didn't have to wait long. Our chief had serious clout. When I heard the motorbike revving up to the Center's doorstep, I clambered to my feet, pulled Muku into my arms, locked the door, and seated myself properly on the bike, as a lady should: side-saddle, gripping the chrome fittings alongside the seat rather than the male motorcyclist's waist.

Off we went, rattling across the pitted rock escarpment surrounding the Center, bumping up the edge of an unpaved feeder road, and turning onto the two-lane, trans-Flores highway.

"*Ke mana?* Where to?" The driver asked.

"*One sekang tua golo* — to the chief's house," I responded.

Of course, the driver wants to know what happened.

"*Saya di injak oleh gajah* — an elephant stomped on me," I yelled into his ear, so he could hear me above the wind, and we shared a laugh, the motorcycle whizzing by rice terraces, thatched houses, and wallowing water buffalo, eventually straining up the dirt road back home.

Rangong.

RrrrrrANGG-ong.

---

1. Also known as a whip spider, although not a true spider or scorpion, but another type of arachnid with a separate scientific classification.
2. A short video of Kanisius in the Tado Community Research Center with the water boatman specimens can be found at https://www.youtube.com/watch?v=HVgYLH9icBA
3. Schleichera oleosa or cambi in Manggarai.

# MANNA

Kenneth P. Gurney

The Coca-cola can tossed from the passing station wagon
scuds across the pavement into the gravel shoulder
and stops in the grass near my hiking boots
where the continental divide trail emerges from the pines
to cross the two-lane state highway.
The soda can fizzy-bleeds its dark brown liquid
from a tiny puncture where the broken pop-top
requires a real opening.
I bend my pack laden back to pick it up
so my Swiss army knife may ram through the aluminum
and I may quench a twelve mile thirst,
knowing I have ten miles to go before camp.

# HOLY WATER
Karen Fayeth

San Francisco's fog chilled the early April morning as Father Pacheco wrapped tighter into his cozy wool blanket and began snoring. His eyes played back and forth under his lids as he dreamed the kind of dream a sleeper wishes would never end. He was a young man again, and his joints did not ache. Long limber legs stood firmly on the deck of his small fishing boat at Puerto Ensenada as he tended to his nets.

He whistled a childhood tune as he worked, but the dream took a dark turn. A rogue wave rushed to shore as the boat swayed and bucked violently beneath him. Panic clutched his heart as he emerged through the long black tunnel into consciousness. His eyes blinked as he struggled to remember where he was, then he startled as a water jug crashed to the floor.

The ground beneath his bed moved on its own.

*"Madre de Dios!"* he shouted, searching frantically for his rosary beads and praying to the Lord Almighty to end his terror.

He was certain this was punishment because in his dream he was not alone. The doe-eyed Felicia Sanchez was with him, and he'd had feelings that a man of the cloth should not feel. He was certain his vengeful god was doling out a just punishment for a wayward priest because this was not the first time he'd had such a dream. Father Pacheco whispered his confession, an apology to the heavens, as the rumbling finally slowed and the earth rested.

It was then that he realized the ground had shaken with a powerful earthquake. Father Pacheco rose from his bed and dressed quickly. As the mission's pastor, he must ensure that all souls in the parish were safe and that the parish itself was secure.

He rustled down the hallway, quickly tying a purple sash

about his waist. Wall sconces had fallen to the ground, but the candle flames had extinguished on impact. He went first to the sanctuary and noticed a few cracks in the thick adobe walls, but the building was structurally sound. Father Pacheco checked the tabernacle and confirmed that the chalice and Host were safe.

He made his way down corridors, out the door and across the street, arriving at the convent to find the women in a state of hysteria.

"Mother Superior!" he shouted sharply. "Gain control of your charges. We must provide aid to the injured! Come quickly!"

"Father Pacheco, the city is ablaze!"

"Yes, Mother Superior. Are your nuns all accounted for?"

"Yes, Father," she replied.

"Then follow me. We must see about the others."

Father Pacheco and Mother Superior walked the length and breadth of the mission and to their relief all souls were safe. They went outside and found the sky above San Francisco had gone gray with smoke.

"Our mission is safe, Mother, but we must keep it that way. Gather everyone in the chapel."

---

Over the next days, the inhabitants of Mission Delores watched in horror as the winds drove blazing fires in their direction. The fire brigade arrived ahead of the flames, and weary firefighters advised Father Pacheco that they could save the mission by dynamiting the nearby structures in an effort to control the burn.

Feeling helpless as the firemen worked, the Father made use of a humble wooden bucket that carried water inside for Mass. He filled it repeatedly from the well pump, quickly blessing the water and pouring it at the base of the mission's structure. It was a small act against a big fire.

His face was covered in soot and tears as he watched the ravenous fire monster devour each nearby building with flames and the firemen fight to keep the flames from progressing. He clung to the bucket as if it were his only savior in a sea of tragedy and chaos. He carried the heavy vessel like a wooden cross, a burden for his sins.

Over and over, he returned to the well to fill the bucket with lifesaving water. He poured it on deadly flames that now licked and stretched to reach the doorstep of the mission.

Father Pacheco screamed out in anger and ran to fill the bucket again, weary arms lifting it once more to extinguish flames. When the bottom edge of the wooden bucket caught a wisp of flame, Father Pacheco felt the scorching blaze of hell on his skin as his demons within roared in syncopation with the demons of fire.

After three days that seemed an eternity, Saturday morning dawned anew. The sun brought its own fire to the world, lighting the devastation below and bringing the uncontrolled damage into bas-relief.

Father Pacheco awoke to find the charred wooden bucket clutched in his arms. It was his penance and his saving grace. He leapt from the bed after only a few hours sleep and ran straight to the well pump to fill the vessel once more, but this final bucketful of water was not necessary.

The fire brigade had won, the flames had ceased, and the destruction had ended. The mission was saved, but the city lay smoldering at the base of San Francisco's seven hills.

Father Pacheco was proud that he had helped save his parish but ashamed at the feelings he'd felt as he poured bucket after bucket of water onto flames. He wondered if San Francisco had paid for the bawdy sins of her people just as the charred skin on his arms was penance for his own. Had each been served a reckoning?

As the morning dawned on April 21, 1906, Father Pacheco

realized fully he was not cut out to be a priest. With the last bucket of water in his hands, he poured it over his head, rebaptizing himself as a new soul.

Just as San Francisco would return to glory, so Juan Pacheco would rebuild his life. That pail of water had christened him a humble fisherman. He returned to Ensenada and fished fertile waters with his doe-eyed bride at his side and his four sturdy sons to continue the family name.

Father Pacheco was born by the water, baptized in water, saved lives with water, and found relief from his demons by returning to the holiest of waters to find his peace.

# HSI-WEI AND THE GOOD
Robert Wexelblatt

It was high summer when Hsi-wei arrived in Bianzhou. He was footsore, thirsty, and troubled by the suffering he had observed in the counties through which he had passed on his way to the capital. In Qi, Tongxu, and Weishi, the peasants grumbled, both the poor and the well-off. In Lamkao, Hsi-wei agreed to take two apples in payment for a little pair of straw sandals. "They're for my grandson, Bo-jing. He's just learned to walk," said the old woman. Hsi-wei asked how things were. "Too much rain, then too little," she explained tersely. "We had some relief, but now they've made these new taxes it's worse than ever." People were hungry and angry.

In accord with Emperor Wen's reorganization, the prefectural administration had recently been moved to Xingyanjun and it was here that his old schoolmate, Lu Guo-liang, lived. It had been nearly a year since Hsi-wei received, in a roundabout way, a surprising letter from him. He and Lu had not been close; in fact, though far from the worst, Lu had been among those who looked down on the upstart peasant who had refused gold for his service and had asked instead to be educated. Lu had enclosed his letter inside one to the painter Ko Qing-zhao, another former classmate, but one with whom Hsi-wei had been good friends and with whom he intermittently corresponded. Lu's letter reached the vagabond poet enclosed in one from Ko. Lu wrote of his marriage and his appointment to an important administrative post in Bianzhou. He offered Hsi-wei a hospitable welcome, should he find himself in the vicinity, adding that he had heard of the growing reputation of the peasant/poet. "I well remember how Master Shen Kuo used to chide you for your calligraphy. If I recall correctly, he once compared your brushwork to what a regiment of grass lizards would leave behind if they'd splashed through a puddle of ink then tramped across a sheet of paper. The old dragon probably brags about you now."

Hsi-wei noticed the contrast between the countryside and Xingyanjun at once. While the peasants were ill-fed, ill-clothed, and ill-tempered here, though there were the usual beggars, most people looked nourished, decently dressed, and busy. When he accosted a robed official in a high hat and asked the way to the villa of the Secretary to the Deputy Governor, the fellow looked at him suspiciously. Should he deign to answer a dusty vagabond with a pack on his back?

"And why would the likes of you be looking for Secretary Lu?"

"To pay the visit he requested me to make, Sir."

The official scoffed and made to move off, but Hsi-wei stopped him.

"Perhaps you would care to see his letter?"

"You expect me to believe a peasant receives letters from a First Secretary?"

"One who can read them as well, Your Honor," replied Hsi-wei tartly and handed over the scroll. The official took it reluctantly and then unrolled and skimmed it.

"Who's this Master Shen Kuo?"

"The teacher of the First Secretary."

"And of *you*?"

Hsi-wei wearied of this tedious conversation. "Sir, can you tell me the way or not?"

The official drew himself up. "Very well," he said. His directions were complicated, perhaps even more than necessary. "And you can tell Secretary Lu that Under-Assessor Hsieh showed you the way."

Night was falling when Hsi-wei found Lu's villa. It was an

old-fashioned place, not notably large but sturdy and dignified, with weathered walls, thick beams, two wide windows and a red door, at which Hsi-wei knocked.

The door was partially opened by a stout female servant who looked Hsi-wei over in a way that was not unfriendly but cautious.

"I'm here to pay my respects to Secretary Lu, at his invitation."

"Secretary Lu is not yet home."

A young woman came up behind the servant. She was pregnant. The wife. Looking anxiously over her shoulder was a thin old woman. Lu's mother. "Go away," she said. "Send that man away."

Lu's wife replied calmly, "Mother, he says he was invited. If we send him away, Guo-liang might be angry."

"Invited? An obvious lie. Guo-liang wouldn't invite a peasant here, not ever, and certainly not as things are now."

"Mei, please let him in," said the pregnant wife.

The servant smiled at Hsi-wei and opened the door.

The mother gave a little yelp of frustration and Hsi-wei could see this was a small skirmish in a long struggle between the women of Lu's household. Such wars are a tradition; not for nothing is the character for strife two women beneath one roof.

"My husband is expected at any minute," said the wife. She spoke graciously, perhaps to spite her mother-in-law; but Hsi-wei could see that, taking in his rough, soiled clothes, the woman was perplexed and a little concerned.

In the background, the old woman growled. "Close the door. Can't you see he's a robber? He'll slit our throats," growled the old woman.

Hsi-wei bowed deeply and addressed the wife. "My name is Chen Hsi-wei. Your husband and I knew each other ten years ago in Daxing."

"In Daxing?"

"As students."

"Chen Hsi-wei?" the wife repeated then broke into a smile. "Oh, the poet. My husband spoke about you. He said he'd sent you a letter, but that was long ago."

"The letter took a while to reach me, and then I was not close by. If you like, I can return tomorrow."

The woman hesitated then said, "Please, Sir. Come in. Mei, fetch us some tea."

The old woman raised her voice. "Daughter, what can you be thinking? He's a stranger, a peasant? Just look at him."

"Enough, Mother," said the wife evenly. With a cry of protest, the old woman retreated inside the house, clutching her robe tightly. Hsi-wei never saw her again, not even at dinner, which was served shortly after Lu came home.

With apparent delight and a bit of irony, the silk-robed Lu greeted Hsi-wei effusively. "Chen Hsi-wei. Is it really you? Yes, of course. Same face, same weight, too, I notice. So, you got my letter? Well, it's a pleasure to see you. I hope you'll be able to grace us with your presence for a day or two? I'd like to introduce you to my superior." Then, to his wife, he said, "Wouldn't you say our peasant/poet looks the part? Order Mei to prepare the spare room."

As soon as they sat down to eat, Lu began to reminisce about their days in Daxing, speaking as if they'd been the best of friends, telling his wife how badly Master Shen had dealt with Hsi-wei and claiming that he had been treated with the same brutality.

"Congratulations on your position," Hsi-wei said to Lu, then, to his wife, "and on the child. I hope you are well?"

"Perfectly well, thank you."

"Yes," said Lu with satisfaction. "I think I can say that I'm a fortunate man."

"You enjoy your work?"

"Very much indeed," said Lu. "My superior, Deputy

Governor Du, an excellent man, is not only wise but decisive. And we've a great deal to do, now that he's become Acting Governor."

"The peasants I saw on the way are suffering."

"Yes. That's regrettable, but there's a crisis."

Lu didn't inquire about Hsi-wei's departure from the capital, his ten years on the road, or his poems; however, he spoke with relish about the emergency with which he was assisting his superior who was now Acting Governor. He went on at length, taking pleasure in the details.

"Of course, the source of our difficulties is the weather. Floods in early spring gave way to drought in early summer. Crops failed. But the problem was compounded by the mistaken policy of our soft-hearted Governor, Hou Bo-qin."

"I've heard about the weather, but not Governor Hou's policy, nor why he's been replaced by your superior."

"The latter's simply explained. When the governors of all the prefectures were summoned to the capital to be informed about the new administrative arrangements, of course Governor Hou, though in frail health, undertook the journey. But, on the way back, he fell ill and was taken to Chiangling where he's been ever since, hovering between life and death. Before he left, though, Governor Hou took an unfortunate measure. He declared that, in view of the hard times, the tax on grain, the *zu*, would be cut in half. He went still further and suspended the tax on textiles as well, the *diao*. The consequence for our city has been catastrophic."

"But," said Hsi-wei, "the people in the city look well-fed and they're not wanting for clothes either. It's the peasants who are famished and in rags."

Lu smiled condescendingly and raised his forefinger, a gesture Hsi-wei recognized, as it was often used by Master Shen.

"That's so, but only because of our store houses. To give him his due, Governor Hou kept them full. However, the populace has been eating through the stores for months and now they're nearly exhausted. You see the problem?"

Hsi-wei did. He also foresaw what Secretary Lu and his admired superior would be likely to do about it. He reviewed what he knew of the Empire's method of taxation, the so-called Equal Field System. The word *equal* seemed to suggest something equitable but, in Hsi-wei's view, that is just what it was not. The officials he knew at Daxing and those he had encountered during his travels all approved of this system and believed it was good for the Emperor's military needs and his vast civil projects. Hsi-wei, however, assessed it with the soul of a peasant.

Under the prevailing system, the unit of taxation was the household. All peasant households—no matter how prosperous or poor—had to pay the same tax. Nobles and high officials were exempt. Those peasants who had no household, a considerable portion, paid no tax in grain or textiles. They subsisted by working for the rich landowners as servants, laborers, or tenant farmers. But there was a third tax in addition to the *zu* and *diao*, a tax all had to pay, the *yong*. Every peasant owed the Emperor twenty days out of the year to be paid in either military service or labor on the Grand Canal. More returned from the former than the latter.

"And what does Acting Governor Du propose?"

"As I told you, he's wise and decisive. The moment he received word of Governor Hou's incapacity, he revoked the ruinous tax remissions and, in consideration of the impending crisis in the city, he increased the grain tax by half. To this urgent measure, he added a long overdue innovation, which shows his genius. It's aimed at the fat landlords. They're all to pay a head tax."

"A head tax?"

"That's right. So much for every servant, worker, and tenant farmer."

Hsi-wei, controlling himself with some difficulty, said sharply, "But doesn't he realize that the well-off landowners will simply dismiss their landless dependents."

Lu rubbed his belly. "Oh, don't believe it. They can't do without their servants and the others. They'll pay up. Anyway, they all have secret storehouses of their own, no doubt crammed with rice and millet—yes, and good cloth, apples, and root vegetables, too."

Hsi-wei was indignant. "So, the plan is to rob the peasants to feed the city?"

Lu frowned. "You put the matter in the worst way, Hsi-wei. There's no robbery. As Acting Governing Du has explained, it's the social and economic function of the peasantry to support the higher culture of the cities. In the same way, the country supports the Court and the Emperor himself. It's regrettable that peasants suffer when the weather goes against them and the harvest is wanting. But it's in the natural order, as is the precedence of the city over the countryside."

Hsi-wei forced himself to stay still for a few moments, though he would have liked to shake his complacent host.

"You said Acting Governor Du is a good man?"

"It's a privilege to serve him."

"And his motives are virtuous?"

"Certainly. He always acts out of duty."

"Only that?"

"What do you mean?"

"Consider our old Master Shen Kuo."

"What's he got to do with it?"

"When Master Shen ridiculed us, when he beat me, don't you suppose he too believed he was doing his duty?"

"Very likely. So what?"

"You didn't observe the pleasure he took in tyrannizing over us? You never noticed the old man's lust for power?"

Lu gaped at Hsi-wei.

"You've heard the saying that we love the good?"

"Something from one of the sages, I suppose. I can't recall which."

"Do you think that sage was blind to all the evil done in the world?"

Lu's face darkened. The two men faced each other alone. Lu's wife had excused herself long before, and her mother-in-law had never come out of hiding.

"You mean to impugn our Acting Governor?"

"No. Merely to understand him. When I arrived, you said I hadn't changed. Neither have you, Guo-liang. You flatter your superior and are indifferent to the suffering he imposes on the peasants. It was just the same in Daxing."

With that, Lu struck the table.

Hsi-wei got to his feet. "Thank you for this meal, which I regret eating and will have a hard time digesting."

Then the poet took up his pack and went out into the dark city.

Hsi-wei spent the rest of the evening walking the city's streets. He slept a little on the grounds of a small Buddhist temple. When dawn broke, he headed into the countryside. In Tongxu, he paid a peasant family for lodging in their shed by making them all straw sandals. Po Ling-xi, the father, was a good man and took to the sympathetic sandal-maker. He confided that, when they learned of the new taxes, the people had gathered what grain they had left and filled clay jars which they buried on the wooded hillsides. They also chose representatives to carry an appeal to the new governor. The wealthiest landlords put themselves forward. Hsi-wei was still in Tongxu when these suppliants were beaten and thrown in prison. Du then ordered troops into the rural areas to confiscate the grain he was certain the peasants had in abundance. When his troops returned empty-handed, he was infuriated and declared that he would burn villages until the grain was forthcoming.

Those convinced of their own virtue are always the hardest to dissuade. In fact, it is rare that foolish self-righteousness is corrected or its bad deeds forestalled. But that is what happened in Bianzhou. Hsi-wei had been on the road south for a week when the news from Xingyanjun reached him.

Governor Hou had recovered and arrived from Chiangling before the troops fired the first village and before the desperate peasants grabbed their rakes and scythes to resist. The first thing the Governor did was to rescind the new taxes. The second was to have his deputy transferred to the far west. The third was to reinstate his lenient tax policy, except now he eliminated the grain tax altogether. These things were easily accomplished. But the problems of famine and the taxes owed the state remained and called for real ingenuity. What Governor Hou did was add ten days to the labor tax. He then used this measure to barter for grain from Jingzhou, which had a surplus, as he had learned in the capital. In return, the labor tax there was cut by the ten days added in Bianzhou. The Emperor was not cheated.

"Hardly perfect," mused Hsi-wei, "but not bad either."

Being a modest poet, Hsi-wei would probably not have rendered a better judgment on the verses inspired by his visit to Bianzhou. The poem has become popularly known as "We Love the Good."

*Even sober, Heng thought it good to revenge himself*
*by murdering Lin who'd insulted him right in the tavern.*
*Didn't everybody detest that troublesome braggart, that sot?*
*Didn't everyone know Lin beat his wife and cheated at weiqi?*

*Captain Fu was sure it would be good not to wait for*
*the reinforcements promised by General Shao*
*but rather to attack at the hour just before dawn.*
*The enemy would still be asleep, their pickets drowsing.*

*The Emperor's nephew resolved it would good to remove
the Son of Heaven. He could rule far more wisely.
He would economize, take fewer concubines, win wars,
appoint less corrupt ministers. The peasants would adore him.*

*Bai-du was certain it would be good to leave the garlic
frying in her wok a little longer, just one more minute
so the cloves would soften and turn a deeper brown.
Then the dish would taste sweet rather than harsh.*

*Heng was dragged weeping to his execution. The would-be
usurper was stripped and beheaded, his wives and lands seized.
Before the sun was up, Fu led his men into a lethal trap.
Bai-du scorched the garlic and ruined her husband's dinner.*

*We love the good, says the sage, meaning all, no exceptions.
He didn't need to add that most of us are sleepwalkers
all-too-certain of our crooked ways, or that, should we wake,
each of us would swear that next time we'll know better.*

# WHOSE FAULT?
Lenny Levine

"They should shut down that Memorial Sloan Kettering Hospital," said the guy next to me in the aisle seat. He weighed 350 if he weighed an ounce, and it was a great effort to keep my leg from coming into contact with his. And this was going to be a five-hour flight.

His name was Sam Pennington. He'd informed me of that shortly after takeoff. He said he was a futures trader for some company I'd never heard of, and he was flying to New York to visit his brother, who lived in Queens.

I, of course, compelled by the niceties of travel, had to tell him my name and the reason I was here in this unfortunate seat.

"Bill Simmons," I said. "I'm going to see my mother. She's at Memorial Sloan Kettering Hospital."

And that's when he opined that they should shut it down.

"Huh?" I said.

He angled his bulk toward me. "Do you know how many people die of cancer inside that building every day? It's a death factory. They should close it down."

Unable to frame a reply, I glanced at the passenger on my other side, a beautiful young woman in the window seat, someone with whom I'd hoped to strike up a conversation. I saw that she'd pulled down the window shade and was, apparently, asleep.

"You think I'm crazy, don't you?" said Sam Pennington.

"No, no," I lied.

"Sure you do. That's why the world is so screwed up."

"Ah."

I opened the paperback in my lap, the one I'd bought at

the airport kiosk. It was *11/22/63*, Stephen King's time-travel fantasy about the JFK assassination. "I think I'm going to read for a while," I told Sam Pennington. *Maybe, for the next five hours,* I thought.

"Sure, sure, don't let me disturb you. That's supposed to be a good book."

"It is, so far."

"But, you know?" He shifted his weight, making my seat move slightly. "I wish people would finally let go of it already."

I couldn't help myself. I asked what he meant, although I knew I shouldn't. And I was right.

"They've got to stop blaming Oswald."

*Okay,* I thought, *he's just your average conspiracy buff.*

"So, you don't think he did it," I said.

"No, of course, he did it. He killed Kennedy in cold blood, no doubt about that. But it's been over fifty years now. Isn't it time people stopped blaming him for it?"

I tried to wrap my mind around this but couldn't.

"So, by the same logic," I said, "it's time people stopped blaming Hitler for the Holocaust?"

He shrugged. "Sure."

I groped for words, then settled on: "That's very interesting."

"Thank you," he said.

Struggling not to roll my eyes, I plunged back into the relative sanity of a Stephen King novel.

But I couldn't concentrate. I kept thinking about my mother, the woman I couldn't wait to get away from three years ago when I'd moved to L.A. to find fame and fortune as a screenwriter.

So far, I've found neither. There's been occasional TV work. You can see my name at the end of a couple of NCIS shows if you look really quickly at the credits flipping by. Aside from that, and some passing interest by an agent in a screenplay I wrote, there isn't much.

I wish I could say we parted on good terms, my mother and I, but we didn't. Her last words to me were, "Go ahead, be a lowlife asshole like your father."

My dad had made his own escape a couple of years earlier and is now living in Boston, happily remarried.

After I moved, I did manage to speak with her on the phone a couple of times, conversations that were rigidly civil with a decided undertone of antipathy. Lately, all of my contact had been with my older sister, Charlotte, who always got along with her better than I did.

I had no idea my mother was sick until last night. Charlotte called me out of the blue with the news that she had stage-four lung cancer. It was like a punch in the heart.

"Oh my God!" I said. "She's always been a heavy smoker, but still…"

"*But still* is exactly right," Charlotte said, sounding eerily like our mother. "They say stress contributes to cancer, and I've seen it up close and personal. She's never been the same, you know, since you left. She can't get over the fact that you defied her. It eats at her every day."

It was like a second punch in the heart.

"You're blaming me?" I said incredulously.

There was an awkward pause. Then: "I think you should come home. Don't worry, it probably won't be for long."

And that's why I couldn't concentrate on Stephen King.

I decided to emulate the beautiful woman on my left and close my eyes for a while. I didn't expect to sleep, but I found myself dozing, a blissful state that was interrupted by Sam Pennington's voice.

"Yes!" he cried out.

My eyes popped open and I looked over at him. He'd lowered the tray table and put his laptop on it. He was now staring contentedly at the screen.

"Yes!" he said again, then seemed to notice I was awake.

"Oh, sorry, I didn't mean to disturb you. I was just reacting to the news that gold is tanking."

"And that's a good thing?" I asked.

"For me it is."

"Ah."

"Let me ask you something." He shifted in his seat and, again, caused mine to move. "What do you think of the service on this flight?"

"I don't know. So far, there hasn't been any."

"You got that right. Flying nowadays is no better than taking a bus. They served meals, once upon a time, not very good ones, but they were free. Now, either you starve or you have to pay five bucks for a bag of pretzels. And you know whose fault that is?"

"The airlines?"

"No, the flight attendants. They wanted more money, so instead, the airlines make them work less."

I had the thought that flight attendants would have to work all day and night if they had to feed him.

"Ah," I said. It was becoming my mantra.

*Bing!* The seat belt sign lit up. A chipper female voice came on the intercom.

"Hi, folks. The captain has informed us that we're going to run into some turbulence, so he's turned on the *Fasten Seat Belt* sign. Please remain seated with your belts securely fastened until the sign has been turned off, which, hopefully, will be soon. Thank you."

"Mmf," said Sam Pennington, pivoting back and forth as he rooted around on both sides of his massive self, trying to find the two ends. I had to duck away a couple of times from flying elbows.

The lovely woman to my left was, incredibly, still asleep, her long, auburn hair covering her cheek, her lips slightly apart. I thought maybe I could break the ice by gently waking her and telling her of the latest seatbelt developments, but I saw that she still had hers fastened.

The plane suddenly heaved violently to the right. Then left. Then, for one horrible second, it dropped like an elevator. My stomach said hello to my throat as I clenched my fists and held my breath. Somewhere behind us, a woman screamed.

"Son of a bitch pilot," Sam Pennington muttered, "taking us for a joy ride. These guys are all cowboys. They just love to show off."

"You think he's doing this on purpose?" I said.

"Of course he is."

The plane bounced, producing another scream from behind us.

"Wha…what's happening?" The beautiful woman, who must have been some good sleeper, had finally awakened. Her eyes, now open, were big and brown, and wide with fear.

"It's only turbulence," I said. "It's okay."

"Turbulence? Are you sure? It felt like there was some kind of explosion." She looked around desperately, trying to see past Sam Pennington, who was grimly holding on to the tray table and his laptop.

"No, no. It's probably because you were asleep. So, you thought—"

The plane bounced again, then moved sideways. This time, the scream didn't come from behind us. It came from her.

"I've got to get out of here!" she said.

It was insanity, of course, but panic knows no reason. Before I could speak, she'd undone her seat belt and was attempting to climb over me. I had no idea how she intended to get past Sam Pennington, who was looking at her with a sort of shocked amusement, but her knee dug painfully into my thigh as she struggled.

"Hey, hey, it's all right, relax," I said, trying to pull her back into her seat.

The plane tilted sickeningly to the left, which did the job for me. It virtually deposited her in the seat, which, of course, did nothing to calm her.

"We're going to die!" she wailed, trying to get up again.

I reached over with both hands and tried to hold her in place by her shoulders, which wasn't easy because I could barely rotate my body in the damn seat belt. But somehow, I had to break through her hysteria.

"Look at me!" I yelled at her. "Look at me!"

She blinked in surprise, but did so.

"I've been through much worse than this," I said, my eyes locked in on hers, forcing her to keep looking at me. "This is nothing, it's just normal turbulence. It's like an amusement park roller coaster. Scary, but no one's going to be hurt. It's no big deal, nothing to worry about."

It was dialogue I'd written for an unsuccessful TV movie. As it happens, the character dies right after saying these lines, along with everyone else, since the story is about an air disaster, but it was all I could come up with. And it seemed to work.

She managed a weak smile. "I hate roller coasters."

"So do I, but we're getting a little extra for our money," I said as I reluctantly let go of her shoulders. She sank back into the seat.

The plane slid to the side again and she gasped.

"It's okay, it's okay," I said as the plane made a hop, skip. "Why don't you put your seatbelt back on?"

Her hands were shaking so much that she couldn't do it, so I did it for her.

"There we go."

She grabbed hold of my hands. "I'm just so frightened. I'm sorry."

"Hey, I know the feeling. No blame, no shame."

Where all this courage was coming from I had no idea. I'd never been in turbulence that was nearly this bone-rattling and brutal. It was terrifying.

Maybe if she'd been fat and ugly, I would've been as scared as she was. And pissed off at her as well, for panicking. But beauty works wonders and, evidently, so does false bravado.

"Do you mind if I hold on to you?" she said, clutching tighter. "I know it's silly, but…"

"No, no, please, that's fine," I told her. "Just let me take one hand away, though, so I can sit up straight."

"Oh, I'm sorry." Her face flushed, which, if anything, made her prettier.

She let go of my right hand, and I sat back in my seat, my left hand nestled warmly in both of hers. Painfully, too, because she was squeezing the crap out of it.

And even worse, there it was, sitting brightly above one of her white knuckles. An engagement ring.

"I would've slapped her in the face," Sam Pennington hissed in my right ear.

"Excuse me?"

"She was panicking. That's how you deal with people like that. The way you're doing it now makes her feel like it's okay to act that way. She'd better not lose it again or it'll be on you."

"Ah."

So there I sat, strapped to my seat. On one side was a 350-pound lunatic. On the other was someone else's fiancée, who was, at present, crushing my fingers to a pulp. If these were to be my final moments, was I fated to spend them like this?

The plane gave another nauseating dip, provoking screams all around us.

I turned toward the bride-to-be, who was staring grimly at the seat cushion ahead, her jaw clenched almost as tightly as her hands.

"My mother hates me," I told her. "And now she's got cancer, so she's going to die hating me. But it's not my fault."

It was as if I'd pulled her out of a reverie. She stared blankly at me. "What did you say?"

"I said my mother hates me but it's not my fault. I just wanted someone to know that."

"Okay, whatever," she said, then went back to staring ahead, her grip on my hand tightening. I had to do something.

"I hate to bother you, but could you ease up a little?"

"Huh?" Her eyes flashed in annoyance. I guess she was praying and I was interrupting her.

"My hand. You're kind of squeezing it pretty hard."

"Oh, right," she said distractedly. She loosened her grip, but not by much.

"I appreciate it," I said, wincing.

The plane did another buck and slide.

"They should slap the damn airlines with a class-action lawsuit," offered Sam Pennington. "For reckless endangerment."

I ignored him and closed my eyes. *Oh, God*, I thought, because why not? *If you really exist…*

But I didn't have time to finish whatever it was I was about to pray because it was over, just like that. The plane steadied and everything became smooth again.

In a few seconds, the seatbelt sign was turned off, and sounds of relief filled the air around me.

She let go of my hand, and I flexed it a time or two. No apparent damage.

Sam Pennington heaved himself out of his seat. "Toodle-oo," he sang out to no one in particular, "I'm off to the loo."

"I don't know how to thank you," the beautiful betrothed lady said to me. "You were incredible. You literally saved me from going crazy. I owe so much to you, and I don't even know your name."

"Bill Simmons," I told her.

"I'm Daisy McCann." We shook hands delicately. "That was some experience."

"Sure was," I said. "Is your fiancé meeting you at the airport?"

"My fiancé? I don't…oh, this." She looked down at the ring on her finger and gave a self-conscious smile. "I forgot that I wear this when I'm traveling alone. It's sort of a protective device, but I don't think I need it right now." To my astonishment, she slid the ring off and put it into her jeans' pocket.

"And I'm so sorry I was rude to you. You were telling me something about your mother, and I just blew you off. That was terrible."

"No, I don't blame you. When you think you're about to die, it's hard to think about anything else."

"But you said she hates you. How can that be?"

"It's just how my mother is," I told her. "She hates everything, so why not include me? She made my father's life miserable, and my sister is the only person on earth who can stand her. In my head, I know I had nothing to do with her being that way; she's always been that way. But now that she's dying, I can't help feeling responsible for her. Like it was, somehow, my fault."

"Is it because you thought it was up to you to make her better, but you couldn't?" Daisy asked me.

I nodded. "Something along those lines."

She reached over and squeezed my hand, gently this time.

"I've been there. As someone once told me, and I think it was you, 'No blame, no shame.'"

From then on, except for the seat-shuddering return of Sam Pennington, we had nothing but clear skies.

# STRANGERS ON A TRAIN
James B. Nicola

He has been looking but has not seen me,
only my clothes and bags. What has gone sour,
and how? I focus on the scenery
to avoid acknowledging the past hour
between us. He looked like a normal man
when first he got on board, but when I said
*Hello!* he snuckered, *Hein, Americain*,
and other exotic sounds. My face turned red.
What could I do but turn to studying
the countryside? In hopes the sound will cease
I nod at every—*nearly* everything
he says and pray he'll let me ride in peace,
the stranger that I am, and not the nation—
at least till I can change my seat, next station.

# THE SWEETEST SOUND
Mary Donaldson-Evans

"Welcome home, Lancelot and Mary!"

Home? The Okavango Delta in Botswana? The smiling African woman who greeted us handed us lavender-scented washcloths and showed us to our "home," a tent that had in common with the pup tents of our scouting days only the fact that it was made of canvas.

The tent, larger by far than the room we had at the Hotel Mercure in London en route over, had a wooden plank floor and a full bathroom. A basket of greenery had been set on the down comforter, in the middle of the queen-sized bed. We pulled back the fronds and leaves and found a bottle of chilled champagne and two champagne flutes with a note that read as follows:

> Dear Lancelot and Mary,
>
> Welcome to Camp Xakanaxa. We hope that you will enjoy your stay with us and let the magic of the Delta touch you in a special way.
>
> If there is anything that you may need, please do not hesitate to ask.
>
> We trust that you will have an enjoyable safari and a memorable stay."

It was signed "Ben, Kago, Hendrick, Loveness, Lorato & CX team."

We uncorked the champagne and filled the flutes. This was indeed going to be the trip of a lifetime.

If only we could master the name game.

As seasoned travelers who once taught French and know a smattering of other languages, my husband and I weren't particularly worried about the linguistic difficulties we'd encounter during our two-week trip. One week would be spent in South Africa, where English is the *lingua franca.* Even if the accent of the Afrikaans-speaking population was at times a bit difficult to understand, we did not anticipate any problems. In Botswana and Zambia, we'd be staying in safari camps accustomed to receiving international tourists. No problem there either.

What we didn't expect, on the other hand, were the challenges that would be presented by proper names. Kago? Loveness? Lorato? How would we remember such names? Now, to be honest, the safari personnel didn't *expect* us to call them by name, even though they used our names with impressive regularity and accuracy. However, as students of Dale Carnegie, we had always done our best to address by name people with whom we had regular contact and, thus, to "win friends and influence people."

Admittedly, our best wasn't always good enough, even in our own culture.

Case in point: at the Y where I work out, I had for two years greeted a man I'd see on the exercise bikes by name. "Hi, David!" I'd sing out every time I saw him. And he'd give me a wan smile and say hello. The fact that he never attempted to learn my name didn't bother me. In fact, it made me feel just a tiny bit superior. Then one day I heard someone call him Mike. I was seized by doubt.

"Is Mike your name?" I asked.

"Yes," he replied.

"I've been calling you David all this time and you haven't corrected me?"

He laughed heartily.

I understood, then, why "David" had never warmed to me,

had always looked at me out of the corner of his eye as if I were a piece of mold that had grown on the bike next to his.

And now, here I was in Africa, confronted by a new and different challenge. If my memory could fail me so spectacularly at home, where I had a whole host of mnemonic devices to help me to recall proper names ("Gene" was "congenial," etc.), how was I going to manage where most of the names were completely unfamiliar?

In truth, the difficulties began well before we reached the first of our three safari camps. In Cape Town, we were greeted at the airport by a woman named Deidre who worked for our travel agent. Where's the other "r" I thought when, at my request, she spelled her name for me. We then met Deon, the man who would serve as our guide and chauffeur during our two-day stay in Cape Town, taking us to Table Mountain the first day and on a tour of the entire southern Cape the second. An unusual name, I thought, but not unheard of. I can do this!

At the airport in Maun, Botswana, where we had flown from Cape Town, two men approached us to inform us that we would be taking a small plane to our first safari camp. Their shirts were embroidered with the name of the camp: Xakanaxa.

"How is that pronounced?" I asked, my experience of words beginning with "x" being limited to xylophone and x-ray.

"Ka-ka-NA-ka" they said, their teeth gleaming.

Knowing the children's word for excrement in French, I winced when I heard the first two syllables. What was the state of the plumbing at these camps?

The men introduced themselves as Charles and Obit. Charles I could deal with, but Obit?

"I wonder if Obit knows what his name means in English," I whispered to Lance after the men had left our side.

"I doubt it, and don't you *dare* tell him," said Lance who, in nearly 48 years of marriage, has sometimes had reason to question my diplomacy.

I remained silent. After a considerable wait, we boarded a small plane and took off for a landing field near Camp Xakanaxa. When we touched down, our luggage was whisked away from us to be taken to our "tent" and we were ushered into a Land Rover for our first game drive. Our driver introduced himself:

"Hi! My name is Chemical."

I thought I had misheard.

"Chemical?" I repeated. "That's your actual name?" I asked.

"Yes, that's the name my mother gave me," he replied in a tone that did not encourage a follow-up question.

I found myself wondering if he had siblings and if they were named in similar fashion. Perhaps there was a Mechanical and an Electrical and maybe even a Civil. Did Chemical's mother subscribe to the "name and destiny" theory? Was she hoping to produce a family of engineers? I didn't ask.

Chemical was clearly no engineer, but he was one heck of a naturalist and driver. He identified animal species and listed their characteristics, their lifespan, told us about their diet, their prey, their predators. Giraffes, elephants, zebras, and lions were easy, but Cape Buffalos? Impalas? Red lechees? Warthogs? So, it wasn't only names of humans that we'd have to commit to memory, but names of animal species as well! Our heads were spinning even before he started naming the birds: magpie shrikes, saddle-billed storks, white-crested helmeted shrikes, fish eagles, ox-peckers, fork-tailed drongos, and more.

Drongos! We exploded in laughter.

"Did you say 'drongo?'" asked my Australian husband.

"Yes," replied Chemical.

Do you know what "drongo" means in Australian slang?"
He didn't.

"It's not a compliment," Lance replied.

Had Chemical taken the time to look up the word in the *Online Slang Dictionary* when he got back to camp, he would have learned that "drongo" means "moron" in Australian slang. The example provided on site would not have earned an *imprimatur* from the feminist brigade: "What a drongo—he dumped a really good-looking Sheila for that sow."

Well, this Sheila felt like a bit of a drongo herself as she struggled to note down the names of all the creatures to which she was introduced. We bounced along the rutted, pot-holed dirt tracks through the delta, ducking to avoid being scraped by the tall grasses and branches that slapped against our vehicle. Is it any wonder my scribbles were illegible? I finally gave up entirely when, after having told us that drivers were instructed not to leave the marked trails, Chemical pulled sharply on the steering wheel and we veered off the path and dove through the grasses, swerving to avoid trees: a leopard had been sighted. Since this was a "special sighting," the rules were laid aside.

We saw her, first slinking through the grass, then on a tree branch. She was majestic and beautiful and we knew her by name. I didn't even need my notebook for this one.

Having triumphed in showing us a leopard on our first game drive, Chemical took us back to camp. And that's when the hard work of memorizing exotic human names began. We took our cue from the Cape Turtle Dove whose cry sounds to the human ear like the admonition to "Work harder! Work harder! Work harder!" It was Chemical who interpreted the bird cry for us.

We knew that there would be bird species we'd never heard of, animals we wouldn't have been able to identify without a guide. What we hadn't expected was the human challenge. Here, everyone addressed us by name. We made quick work of explaining that although all of Lance's registration materials were in the name of "Lancelot Donaldson-Evans," in order to be in conformity with his passport, he had not been called by the name his mother gave him at birth since, well, birth. They didn't need to be told twice.

From then on, it was Lance and Mary. "Good Morning,

Lance and Mary. How are you, Lance and Mary? Did you sleep well, Lance and Mary?" And so on.

This was hospitality at its best. The least we could do was to learn the names of the staff members and others who attended to us.

And so we did. At our second camp, the Chobe Game Lodge, staff members had names that sounded familiar to our ear (for example, our game driver was known as "DK," and we did not complicate life by asking what the letters stood for). But different challenges were in store for us. DK's English was heavily accented, and she was soft-spoken. I strained to hear her commentary. We learned the names of people, plants, and animals. We learned the words for their groupings: a *pack* of wild dogs, a *dazzle* of zebras, a *pride* of lions. When DK spoke of "heads of elephants," I was confused.

"Is that what groups of elephants are called? Heads?" I asked.

"Yes," she replied. And she repeated: "Heads."

"How do you spell that?" I asked, pencil poised.

"H-E-R-D-S" she replied.

To get to our third camp, Toka Leya, we had to take a ferry across the fast-flowing Zambezi River into Zambia. Nawa, the driver who met us on the other side and took us to the camp, was easy to understand, perhaps because there were no competing noises from outside: the van was air-conditioned, the windows closed, and the road paved.

Our journey ended at the riverbank where a small metal boat with an outboard motor awaited us. Mailos, our captain, would also be our principal guide and driver during our stay at Toka Leya.

A warm, slightly plump woman with an infectious laugh greeted us at water's edge.

"Hello, Lancelot and Mary. Welcome to Toka Leya," she said, handing us scented washcloths.

She was wearing a nametag that said "Mwame." Trying to commit it to memory, I asked her what it meant.

"Queen," she said, laughing.

A pleasant middle-aged man named Stephen gave us our orientation. *Whew!* I thought. *A name I'll be able to remember!*

The same could not be said for Odon, who took our lunch order, or Amon, the activities director, who tried to talk us into bungee jumping or at least a helicopter ride over Victoria Falls; or Oman, who worked as a waiter; or Thebe, who cleaned our room. We became hopelessly confused, took Odon for Amon. Amon for Omon. Unfortunately, most staff members did not wear their nametags regularly. Only the names of Stephen, Felix (a restaurant worker) and Mailos, with whom we spent a lot of time, managed to make a dent in the folds of our brain.

Lillian, a weary-looking woman with cloudy eyes, missing teeth, and a three-year-old son who didn't leave her side, guided us through the indigenous village of Sinde. Her name too was easy to remember, not only because it was familiar to our Anglophone ears, but also because it was my mother's name.

On our last day at Toka Leya, we were given a client appreciation form to fill out. In the narrative portion of the form, I singled out several staff members for special mention, including Mwame, who had been friendly and helpful to us throughout our stay. It was only as we were bidding adieu to the staff that I looked at the nametag of a woman I did not recall having seen before: It read "Mwame."

"Mwame?" I asked. Is there another "Mwame"?

"No, just me," she laughed.

"But when we arrived, we were greeted by a woman named Mwame. She said her name meant Queen."

"Yes, that's right!" she said. "It was me. My name means Queen."

The mystery was solved when *my* Mwame rounded a corner. For once, she was wearing her nametag. It read "Thebe."

I rushed back to Stephen's office and changed the name on the client appreciation form.

That embarrassing episode should have given me pause, made me realize that despite my good will, I had not mastered the name game and might as well give up. It didn't.

At the airport in Livingstone, a charming young woman checked us in for our flight. The letters HMNIA were stitched into the pocket of her uniform. Having learned about tribal languages, strange combinations of letters, etc., I was intrigued.

"How is your name pronounced?" I asked.

"Abigail," she responded.

It was then that I noticed that all the agents had uniforms sporting the initials HMNIA. We were, after all, at the Harry Mwanga Nkumbula International Airport.

Some days later, my husband, not to be outdone, could not resist the temptation to comment on the name of a cashier in a shop at the Johannesburg Airport: "Mxlosi."

"How do you pronounce your name?" he asked.

The young man pronounced an M, then clicked his tongue against his teeth the way you'd do if you were trying to encourage a horse to gallop, and then said "Losi."

"Is that a tribal language?" asked Lance.

Mxlosi: "It is."

Lance: "Do many people know how to pronounce it?"

Mxlosi, motioning to the other staff, replied, "Around here, they do."

*Around here they do.*

Ouch! What a lesson for us! We were mere tourists, clearly not from "around here," thus not expected to be able to pronounce the unusual names of this man and his compatriots. We admired the subtlety with which he pointed out our ethnocentrism.

It was time to return to the USA. In just a few hours, we'd be on the plane headed for England, and from there we'd fly home, home to the range, where the buffalo roam and the deer and the antelope play, home where we know animals and people by name. But, before we walked down that drafty jetway, Africa had one more surprise in store for us, one more sign that it had beaten us at the name game.

We had not yet settled in at our gate. I had left my husband seated on a bench, surrounded by our hand luggage, and I was finishing up my souvenir shopping when I heard an announcement:

"Would Mary Donaldson please present herself to the nearest agent?"

I exited the shop and went to find my husband. "What's *that* about?" I asked him.

"Probably nothing. We're in South Africa. There must be dozens of Mary Donaldsons in Johannesburg alone. Besides, that's not your name. Your name is Mary Donaldson-Evans."

"Yeah, you're probably right," I said, unconvinced.

I bent over to gather up my luggage.

"Where's my laptop?"

The laptop was missing.

I rushed to the nearest information kiosk, spying my laptop as I approached. A "nice lady," the agent told me, had turned it in. In the absence of an identification tag, they had searched the pockets of the case and had come upon a torn ticket stub with the name Mary Donaldson still intact.

Suffice it to say that while Dale Carnegie was right about many things, he got it wrong when he insisted on the importance of accuracy. It's not true that we never forgive people who mispronounce, misspell, or otherwise mutilate our names. When your lost laptop is on the other end of the mangled name, it is the sweetest sound in the universe.

# A WORLD OF ETERNAL SILENCE
Alistair Rey

The Cheswick School for the Deaf is situated at the intersection of Croydon and Black Friars Road. To reach the front entrance you have to walk through a narrow stone passageway that opens onto a garden courtyard. The sound of violins and flutes is the first thing you notice emerging from the passage. You may be excused for initially wondering whether the symphonic ensemble is intended for your arrival. However, a quick glance to the right will dispel you of any such notions. The gilded plaque on the building directly opposite the Cheswick School reads Latraud Institute of Music. The two buildings, separated by a shared courtyard, are virtually identical, one a school for the deaf, and the other a music conservatory.

Isn't life peculiar, I think as I ring the bell.

Ms. Grimcass, the governess of Cheswick, is a staid and elderly woman. She is dressed in black giving the impression of having just returned from a wake. Her manner is cordial; one might even say maternal. She smiles and states how wonderful it is that the public has taken an interest in the school before inviting me into a Victorian-style sitting room. Would I like a cup of tea? Or do reporters prefer coffee, she wants to know.

"Tea is fine," I say.

I don't have the heart to tell her "reporter" is technically inaccurate. My designation is the "soft news" bureau.

While Ms. Grimcass is preparing the tea, I notice a young professional-looking woman sitting on a sofa in the adjacent room. "Pleasant day out today, isn't it?" I ask just to make conversation. She doesn't acknowledge my comment.

"Leila can't hear you, Mr. Merrick," Ms. Grimcass says as

she returns with the tea. "She is one of our scholars."

"Oh right..." I reply weakly.

I can hear the musicians in the opposite building rehearsing a work by Handle. It provides a pleasant ambience.

Ms. Grimcass gives me a condensed history of the Cheswick School and I scribble down the pertinent details in my notebook. I consciously try to act journalistic, posing questions and writing down her responses verbatim as if intending to use them for quotes. Soft news rarely uses quotations, but Ms. Grimcass seems pleased with the interview process. My attention is repeatedly distracted by a panel hanging on the opposite wall with the inscription:

> If I regard wickedness in my heart, The Lord will not hear.
> *Psalms 66:18*

When Ms. Grimcass notices my gaze, she smiles. "We here at Cheswick believe that a sound education begins with religious instruction," she states matter-of-factly.

I only nod, scribbling absently in my notebook.

"And how long have you shared the building with the music conservatory?" I ask, changing the subject. I point in the air with my pen as though the music is palpable. In a way, it almost is. It permeates the absolute silence of the building, each dulcet note suffusing the air like a presence in the room.

"Since the early 1920s," Ms. Grimcass informs me. "Lovely, isn't it? All of us here have grown quite fond of the music over the years."

I flash her an awkward smile, unsure whether she is trying to make a joke.

After the interview, I am given a tour of the facilities. Students shuffle through the halls, their heads angled downward and books clutched studiously under their arms. In the classrooms, teachers stand before rows of pupils communicating in sign language and drawing diagrams on chalkboards. The absence of any noise is conspicuous. Everything is mute like a silent film. These scenes are overlaid with the melodies coming from the neighboring music school, now rehearsing a somber piece by Berlioz. The effect is surreal.

On the upper floor, the rooms are designated for speech therapy sessions. More advanced students sit with instructors who demonstrate how to position the lips and tongue to make phonetic sounds. Ms. Grimcass interrupts the class, communicating to the students in a series of hand signals. I assume that she has introduced me and wave.

"I aem pleesd tow meet yoo," one student says to me in slow deliberate speech. "Doo yeu layk ower scool?"

I tell her that I am also pleased to meet her and that I am very impressed with her school. She looks to Ms. Grimcass, confused.

"Ensure that your lip movements are pronounced, Mr. Merrick," she instructs. "This particular student is still learning to read lips."

I repeat the phrase again, articulating each word slowly. The girl smiles. The music students have suddenly switched gears and moved on to a piece in tempo allegro. The transition feels appropriate, but the girl is unaware. I am becoming conscious of what it must be like to live in a world of eternal silence, to never hear your own voice or the verbalization of your own thoughts.

The last wing of the tour is the conference room, now empty. It is a large formal chamber with high ceilings and decorative fixtures. Pale sunlight pours through the eight-foot-high windows located at the opposite end.

"This is one of my favorite rooms in the building," Ms. Grimcass tells me as we walk, our footsteps echoing on the hardwood. "It was designed by Norman Bentley in 1898."

I nod, pretending I know who this is. I recognize the music

coming from the conservatory and pause at the window. It is by Brahms. From my vantage point, the entire courtyard is visible. Cheswick students walk about the grounds below, shrouded in imposed silence. It all seems cruel to me as I rest my elbows on the windowsill and listen to the chorus of violins, oboes, and woodwinds travel across the air. Then, fixing my gaze, I discern the graceful gestures of swinging arms, the synchronized footsteps and almost balletic quality of bodies as they move along the paving stones and between the garden shrubbery. From this elevated perspective, I can see a living symphony unfolding before me.

# THE ACUTE AND THE GRAVE
Scott Dominic Carpenter

"So," my friend Martine asked, "what city do you fly into?"

I was headed for the States, with a first port of call on the eastern seaboard. "Newark," I replied—although, because we were speaking in French, I didn't really say "Newark," but instead replaced that clipped little name with the stretched-limousine version, separating the vowels and turning the metropolis of belching smokestacks into something suddenly svelte: "*Nou-ark.*"

Martine pulled a look, one eyebrow rising as the other dipped. Was it possible she'd never heard of it? I clarified where the place was located: "*Nou-jair-ssay.*"

Her eyes rolled toward the heavens. "*Mon dieu.* I suppose you think that's clever."

She was talking, of all things, about my accent—or rather, about my pretending not to have one. I am, for better or worse, an American, so what business did I have pronouncing words like "Newark" and "New Jersey" à la française? Such names were among the few things I was expected to utter correctly—which is to say, like the Yank I am.

I managed a pinched smile, but in that little notebook I keep tucked in the back of my brain, I jotted a phrase: *See? You can't win.* Most of the time, if you plop an American name or word into a conversation without churning it through the processing plant of French pronunciation, nobody knows what you're talking about. I noticed this long ago, back during the Bush presidency. Hapless but well-intentioned French-speaking Americans faltered in conversations having to do with Dubya. In the American version, the U of *Bush* is so relaxed it has practically gone on vacation, whereas French makes you choose between stark alternatives, turning our man of state into a homonym for *bouche* ("mouth") or *bûche* ("log," or, in slang, "blockhead"). Despite the temptation of the second option, it's the first that gained currency. Nevertheless, a lot of Americans opted for a third option—that is, doing what Martine had told me to do with New Jersey: just blurt the thing out in American. But if you do that, then French people tend to squint and wrinkle their nose. They are lost. Saying "bush" instead of *bouche* or *bûche* is like shifting a beehive six inches while the drones are out: the poor critters never make it home again.

French people have it easy: they routinely Frenchify American names. Americans, though, always have a choice to make: when speaking with a run-of-the-mill Frenchman, you should Frenchify pronunciation for ease of communication; however, if your interlocutor prides himself on his English, you're expected to yokel it out with exaggerated Americanness.

At least most of the time. A little experimentation reveals that the American accent you employ has to be in line with the drone of network news anchors—pretty much what you'd find in central Nebraska. Try dropping *Nawlins* or *Loosiana*—or, for that matter, *New Joy-zee*—into your French, and even the sticklers will start to back down.

It's hard to know how far to take this. Some cases are easy. For instance, after decades of brainwashing by imported crime series, the French have learned to refer to our Federal Bureau of Investigation as the *Eff-Bee-Eye*, and only the most overzealous American would attempt to twist it back to the French letters, *Eff-Bay-Ee*. But what about the ends of those shows, when the crime has been solved—or, even better, thwarted? Then you're in front of a happy ending—a story-telling concept so American that the French have no word of their own for it, calling it *le happy end*—beheading the h of happiness when they say it. What then? Are those of us with US passports all supposed to twang out *happy end* with an American accent, as if people actually use this expression in the New World?

Of course, Americo-Parisians (or Pariso-Americans) get to deal with this both coming and going. Stateside, I hesitate at the American pronunciation of words like *croissant* or *crêpe*. Depending on the situation, I wonder if I've been deputized to carry the banner of false-Frenchness, or if this is one of those occasions where *croy-sant* and *crayp* are more appropriate. The French and English wires often cross in my brain, and as sparks fly, I utter some monstrous twining of the two. If I catch myself in time, I simply choose something else from the menu.

The accent business may not be as big as Google or 3M, but there are legions of French teachers in the US, each one training students to gargle their Rs and squeak their Is. They make a big deal of it. The idea seems to be that when you travel to a foreign land, you should try to fit in. When in Rome, etc., etc. In particular, you should take a stab at the accent.

Unless, of course, your travels don't require you to change languages. We expect students learning German and Chinese to pronounce things like Berliners and Beijingians, but for some reason, when Americans hoof it to Great Britain, taking on the local accent is *verboten*. All it does is turn you into what we call a pompous ass (or, if you prefer, *arse*). Strangely, the reverse does not hold: A Brit coming to the US is allowed to dilute his accent over time and at least partly adopt our own. That's normal enough, I guess: he's finally letting down his hair, no longer feeling compelled to pretend he belongs to the prop department of the BBC.

The accent police may be on patrol everywhere, but their headquarters are definitely in Paris, and they even threaten natives with their billy club of elocution. A friend of mine hails from Narbonne, down near the border with Spain—a place where Rs come with a Spanish trill and vowels hum in the nose. But Thomas speaks like your typical buttoned-down Parisian, only his grin and affability betraying his origins. "I lost it," he said of his native patter, "when I came to Paris." He didn't mean that it went missing, the way you lose an umbrella; no, he had ditched it, the way a criminal tosses evidence into the river as special agents from the Eff-Bee-Eye close in on him.

The problem is going to get worse before it gets—well, let's be honest, it's never going to get better. Languages have always snuck over borders, engaging in eyebrow-raising miscegenation, but you may as well get used to it. These days, thanks to the Internet, and telecommunications, and low-cost airlines, and pretty much everything else, all bets are off. Hordes of words scuttle across those dashed lines on the map, and no wall is going to stop them. It's a fait accompli. At dinner parties, you get button-holed by a guy in *le marketing*, and he yacks about some *nouvelle startup*—one with an exciting *business plan*. It has become de rigueur to discuss *les piercings* of your host's teenage daughter, which make her look like a femme fatale, or *le coming-out* of your co-worker's son. Worse, *les reality shows* on *television* have delivered the coup de grâce to high culture, not to mention haute couture and even haute cuisine. Everywhere you look, the hive has been moved six inches or more, and you realize, finally, that this is what's been killing the bees! And, in the bargain, you.

In such conversations, I attempt to ping-pong between languages and accents, but I don't have the savoir-faire, or else the savoir-vivre, that it requires. I'm missing a little... I don't know...a little... je ne sais quoi. Yes, that's it. So, my pronunciation ends up halfway between Paree and New Joyzee, and as the wrong sounds tumble from my *bouche*, I feel like a *bûche*, or even like George Bush. And that, I can assure you, is no *happy end*.

# THE MYSTERY OF THE STAIRS
George Moore

Easy does not like stairs.
They are the long negotiation
of right paw, left paw, rhythm
of the eternal damnation.

Easy would not make police dog
nor survive in search and rescue.
The ups and down are a mystery
mentally beyond my knowing.

Such is the Hitchcockian dilemma
of Montreal. The third floor
apartment, the 19th-century hall.
And the one flight that links

the cycles of heaven and hell.
Easy does not like stairs.
The invisible creature of self
makes him hesitate, lunge, repeat.

Those things we do without thinking:
washing dishes, cleaning the room,
sweeping endlessly as any Buddha.
Those things we fear only to hesitate

in doing for the mystery of stairs,
the unthought rhythm of our lives.
Easy does not like stairs. He sees
himself in each crocked step

as in a hall of mirrors. Each line
across his colorblind sight
is the self falling through the air.
Each self separated out into now.

Easy does not like stairs. The mystery
of movement, one's own, another's,
the sweeping toward death
at the heart of all action.

For us, for the enemies, for fear
of flight, for the unnatural distance
and the narrow steps of old ladies,
for the sickness at heart,

just to be there, sleeping, standing
above, or below, but not to negotiate,
contemplate, the telescoping selves
into the future.

Easy does not like stairs.
Wouldn't you rather play outside?
Why live at the top of the world
when the passage is all darkness?

The pyramid, the Mayan temple,
the stone steps of Skellig Michael,
the cavern to cavern descent
of Carlsbad.

The earth is flat; the day sunny.
Wouldn't you rather play outside?
The legs ignore the mind,
the last surge, sweeping upward,

rapid as a piano player in a dark hall,
lost in the wonder of his extra-mental
life, never lingering, never thinking
that the thought would make it so,

the journey is forgotten as soon
as it is done, until the morning,
the call, the moment, and then again.
Easy does not like stairs.

# EMILY
Elaine Barnard

I have received a scholarship for English Independent Study at Shandong University in the far city of Jinan. In 1949, Chairman Mao declared such scholarships to encourage literacy among our people. My grandmother worshiped Mao. She had his picture on all the walls of our little farmhouse. Even out back she had his photo above the hole in the ground my father dug for our necessity. Occasionally, I found flyspecks on his cheeks. I brushed them off when I helped Grandmother to the outhouse. She had difficulty walking. Her feet were once bound, which was the custom in her youth. And even though Mao declared that women should unbind their feet, Grandmother's toes never healed properly. She waddled about like ducks in our pond, slipping easily on the muck. I heard her cry for help, her shrill voice pleading for me to come. From then on, I did not allow her to go to the outhouse alone.

Grandmother encouraged me to apply for this scholarship, even though it meant I could no longer care for her. "To learn English is necessary for the young. For me, it does not matter. My brain is weak. But for you, dear Emily, the world is ripe as those persimmons waiting to be peeled."

And so I went, leaving the farm I loved so well, the greenhouse where we raised plump tomatoes, and cucumbers long as my arm, fertilized with droppings from chickens that fluttered about our yard. I traveled on an overnight sleeper. The benches felt hard as stone, six passengers to a compartment, men and women together. Being the youngest and the most limber, they assigned me the top bunk. As I was wearing a skirt, I did not prefer this. Men on lower bunks took advantage of their position, ogling me when I climbed above them. Embarrassed by this, I did not leave my bunk all night, even though I wanted to relieve myself in that dingy toilet at the far end of the train.

In the shrouded morning, we pulled into an unlit station. I lay in my bunk until all the men left, even though they kept offering to help me climb down. I hoped someone from the University would greet me, but no one came. It was very early; the amenities were not open. A lone attendant in blue uniform straggled about with her bamboo broom, collecting cigarette butts littered on the floor, her mouth covered by a white cotton mask, her hands in plastic gloves. I felt as if an unwashed blanket had smothered me, replacing the pure air I breathed at home. My heart ached for home, the cackling chickens, the touch of my grandmother. Even the scolding voices of my parents would have been welcome.

My clothes and hair were rumpled from a sleepless night. Men snored so loudly they even outdid the roaring train. I had never been on a train before. Trains frightened me, even though Grandmother assured me there was nothing to be scared of. "Trains in China are safe. They will not fly off the tracks as they do in America." I tried to control my fear. I would not disgrace Grandmother.

I untied the scarf she had given me as a farewell present and secured it around my mouth to ward off infection. Buses waited outside the station to multiple destinations, but none seemed to be going to Shandong, to the West Campus. The University had many campuses that specialized in particular areas of study. Finally, a slender boy on a rusty bicycle sensed my confusion and offered to take me there. "It's my business." He strapped my belongings on back. "It's not legal, but legal jobs are hard to come by. I invent my own."

A skilled rider, he weaved between cars and buses, carts filled with carrots, cauliflower, huge purple eggplants. and tiny yellow squash. Occasionally, he swiped a squash, passing it to me to slip in his basket, promising to share the booty if I did not report him. "I will never report you. You are the first friend I have made in Jinan."

He gave me a half smile. I could see that one canine was missing, that he tried to conceal it by never smiling fully. In the countryside, dental care was difficult to come by. One must travel many miles to a clinic. I heard such care would be easier to obtain in the city, but perhaps that was just propaganda to lure peasants to the towns for temporary employment on new construction sites.

"I call myself Michael," he hollered as he caught the tail end of a bus. When the bus came to a stop, the driver descended upon him with curses and threats. But Michael pleaded, "I must get this girl to a clinic. She's very sick."

The driver relented. "Be careful. Police are strict in Jinan. They might impound your bicycle." His passengers began to hoot at the delay, so he stomped aboard and drove on amidst the cheering clang of lunch pails.

"Why do you call yourself Michael?" I coughed over the fumes of the departing bus.

"Michael Jackson's cool." He pushed his bike from the curb. "Even when he's hot he's still cool. I want to be like him."

"I heard he used the whitening potion they sell in the market."

"I've tried that stuff. It doesn't work for me, but that's all right. I'm cool in spirit."

I wish I could be cool, I thought, when we hit a puddle left over from the recent rains. It spattered my flip-flops and dirtied my toes. I resembled a migrant worker from my village rather than a student. I felt grateful Grandmother had hidden my new white running shoes inside my clothes roll rather than letting me wear them as I had wished. "You must look smart on campus," she said. "Dirty shoes will make you look stupid."

The buildings were huge in Jinan, almost touching the sky. Some leaned to the side. I feared they would fall upon us. Workers teetered on ladders, pounding and drilling until my ears ached. "Does this go on all day?"

"It never stops. Even by torchlight, it continues."

"How do you stand it?"

"You must try to get used to it, even to love it. It's a sign of prosperity. Soon, we'll be number one."

"My grandmother says the same. She says that time is coming."

"Just read the news, watch the TV. China's on the rise."

"We do not have the television on my farm."

"Then how did your grandmother know all this?"

"My father talks to the tradesmen when he sells our vegetables in the city. He brings back old newspapers. I read them to my grandmother. Her eyes do not work well, but she still knows many things."

"We're here." He swerved the bike to avoid the guards waiting at the University gate. They were busy directing traffic in and out of the sprawling campus. On an adjacent field, students played soccer and volleyball amidst cheers from fans crowding walkways. I could hardly wait to be part of that excitement.

"Wait here." The guard held Michael's handlebars. He could not pass.

"She's a new student," he said. "I'm taking her to her dorm."

"Which dorm you in, Miss?" He peered down at my feet with suspicion.

"I am a scholarship student." I dragged my certificate from my satchel, where it lay buried beneath the books I brought from home, an edition of Shakespeare's plays in Chinese, several novels by the Bronte sisters, particularly Emily, my favorite, and the Nancy Drew mysteries I had read as a child. Simple English helped me to master the language.

"Scholarship students are across street, behind clinic." He inspected my certificate and waved it back to me, unimpressed.

"Behind the clinic? Why am I not on this campus with the other students?"

"University regulations. Scholarship students not regular students."

"What do you mean?'

"They separate group. If you scholarship student, you never be University student."

"I do not believe that."

"You find out."

Michael careened into honking cars.

"Careful." I grabbed the handlebars. An auto screeched its brakes.

"They never wait." Michael rang his bell. "You have to be a tiger."

Feeling a twinge inside, I hugged the crossbar, knees shaking. We cycled into the clinic's courtyard. Freshmen students in khaki uniforms paraded like real soldiers. How I would love to be one of them. How I would cherish such a uniform, even if it meant I must march every day. I would be a true student then, able to afford my tuition, not a hanger-on, a scholarship student from the farm, too poor to afford the University. Being poor in new China seemed a disgrace.

Michael unstrapped my roll and helped me tie it on my back. "I'll carry your books for you." He reached for my satchel.

"I can do it."

"It would please me, Emily." He locked his bike among other bikes, paint peeling, tires threadbare.

"How did you know my name?"

"I guessed. All that Emily Bronte in your satchel. It was either Emily or Nancy. I knew it couldn't be Shakespeare."

"You are right. I will never be that smart."

"I like that name, Emily. It's cool.

"As cool as Michael?"

"Almost."

He danced to the back of the clinic while the freshmen applauded. I followed him to a dirty courtyard strewn with broken cement, lunch wrappers, and beer cans. In the midst of debris stood an isolated building. Air conditioners fronted the windows, increasing the cacophony of the clinic. Clotheslines with girls' panties and pajamas clung to the sides of the collapsing structure.

When we reached the door, he handed me my books. "Good luck in your studies. And don't pay any attention to that gate guard. I don't think he knows what he's talking about."

"Thank you." I pulled some yuan from my satchel, but he hurried off.

Suddenly, he turned, "Maybe I'll see you around."

"Maybe…" A thread of hope filled me. I remembered Grandmother sewing the very dress I wore. I would not let her down.

A heavy rain began to pelt me. I rushed inside to protect my books. Moisture would surely destroy their tattered pages. I had purchased them at a bookstall during one of my infrequent trips to the city with my father where, after a good harvest, I would help him sell vegetables. Returning late, I read by flashlight. Our electricity was sometimes out after a storm, but more often my father chose to cut the power. He was saving money against the next harvest that might fail. He needed to put something aside.

I had not relieved myself for some hours. In desperation, I searched for the nearest toilet. Finally, in an alcove, I saw the sign, W.C. The stench was almost unbearable, but there was no alternative. I squatted above the hole, my feet straddling the sides.

I wanted to clean myself, but there was no water or paper in the cubicle or in the sink outside, a common hand washing area for men and women. Only an old rag hung on a hook, a reminder that at one time the faucet worked.

The hallway was lined with rooms bearing numbers. Boys were on the first two floors, girls on the third and fourth. On the main campus, they had separate buildings. Boys waved, strummed guitars, called to me as I passed. I hurried to the third floor, searching the corridor for room 313.

In the center of the corridor, a large kitchen held a huge water filter and some burners for cooking. Mops and brooms leaned in a corner beside plastic garbage sacks. Empty coke cans escaped an opening. A few peels of onion and garlic littered the counters amidst grains of rice and scraps of steamed bread. My stomach grumbled. I hadn't eaten since yesterday. As I reached for a bite of bread, I heard a voice behind me and turned. A chubby girl stood there with hair as black as mine and glasses so thick that I hardly saw her eyes. She held out her hand.

"You must be Emily. They told me you would be our sixth roommate."

"You are Willow, the one who wrote to me?"

"Don't laugh. My parents hoped I'd grow willowy as Jinan's special tree. It never happened."

She flung my roll over her shoulder. "Our room is beside the staircase. It's noisy. Metal doors make a big bang at night. But you get used to it."

She opened our room. Six bunks adorned the gray walls, one on top of the other. "Since you're last to arrive, you get the top bunk next to an air conditioner. You can use your clothes as a pillow. No closet, only those hooks on the wall."

The room seemed to swell. I thought I must be getting a head cold. I longed for our farm, the cerulean sky afloat with clouds so dense they could be snow cones at the fair.

"Bathroom's down the hall. We take turns for showers. Hot water's only a brief period morning and night." She inspected my toes.

My stomach growled so loud it embarrassed me, but I could not control it.

"You must be hungry. Come, I'll take you to the cafeteria. It's on the main campus. Lunch is almost over, but there should be something left."

She locked our door. "You have to be careful. Theft is rampant."

We clomped our way down an echoing staircase. There was no way one could sneak out of here. We crossed the courtyard. Students played volleyball amidst rubbish. Then we were into traffic. Willow grabbed my hand, dragging me between honking autos and colliding bicycles.

"You have to be a tiger," she chanted. We jostled our way onto the campus.

A thick yellow pall hung over the University. It seemed difficult to discriminate between statues and people. Ghostlike buildings hovered between bare trees. Nearing the cafeteria, bright banners emerged from the pall, flying like signals from another world. Students mobbed tables to sign for fall activities.

"Have you signed?" I asked Willow. She did not answer, so I repeated my question.

"Scholarship students can't join in campus activities, but you get used to it." Her glasses fogged. I had the feeling Willow would never get used to it and neither would I.

"Cafeteria's on four levels." She pushed aside the plastic streamers that deterred insects from entering. "The most expensive food is at top. We'll eat on first level."

The only items left were rice and steamed bread with a few dishes of pickled cabbage. "It's a limited menu down here, but it's cheap. You don't have your food card yet so I'll treat."

"I wish to repay you." I offered some yuan.

Willow pushed them away. "It's my pleasure today. Tomorrow it'll be yours."

We laughed, carrying steamed bread to a table only partially cleared. Chicken bones mixed with slops of vegetable soup and tea. It was late. Workers were eating lunch, paying no attention to debris. "Is it always this messy?"

"You get used to it." Willow flipped a chicken bone to the floor.

Pulling apart the huge white glob of steamed bread, I stuffed it in my mouth the way Willow did. At this time of day, at home, we would be sitting together for our midday lunch of fresh tomatoes and cucumbers, steamed squash and baby carrots, with big bowls of fried rice topped with bits of egg and chicken. How I longed for my mother's cooking.

"Would you like to visit the student market?" she asked, while we chewed the last bits of bread.

We left the cafeteria to workers, who shouted to each other above clattering pots and pans.

The student market was cramped, shelves bursting with everything from Adidas to apples. "I'll leave you here." Willow dropped some oranges into her basket. The clerk weighed them, carefully placing the fruit in a plastic sack and marking the price. Willow waved on her way to the cash register. "I must attend English corner. Can you find your way back?"

"No problem." My stomach churned at the thought of crossing traffic without Willow.

"Well, then, I'll let you explore, but don't be late. Your roommates are cooking dinner tonight. Tomorrow it'll be our turn."

A sense of panic engulfed me among the rows of Lay's potato chips, Hershey bars, and Snyder's pretzels. Most items were imported from America. Suddenly, I heard a clear American voice on the other side of the aisle. How I wished to speak American like the actors I had seen on television when my father took me to the city.

I peeked between boxes of Quaker Oats and Cheerios, Rice Cakes and Fruit Loops. "May I join you?" I whispered, afraid the tall blonde teacher would say no. She already had a circle of students trying to imitate her accent.

"Of course." She smiled, pushing a strand of hair behind a dangling earring. I rushed to the other side of the aisle before she changed her mind.

"What dorm are you in?" She fingered a pretty lavender package of sour plums.

I thought of lying, of pretending I was a regular student, for fear she might dismiss me if she knew the truth. But I must learn to be a tiger. I breathed in hard, then heard myself say, "I live in the Scholarship Dorm, behind the clinic."

"Oh." She opened the package, her fingernails long and delicate, pink as the lotus on our lake. Someday, I will have nails like that, I thought.

"You must be very smart to have a scholarship." she said. And seeing the other students turn their backs to me, she offered me a plum.

# MASSAGED IN VEIN
Sabrina Harris

While vacationing at a remote beach camp on the island of Lombok in Indonesia with my husband, I decided to indulge in a traditional massage of the indigenous Sasak people. Up to that point, everything Sasak—the music, the art, the dancing, the people, the food—had been wonderful. Although looking back, it was all fairly intense: the music loud and frantic, the food spicy, the dancing energetic. The receptionist who booked the massage for me didn't ask any questions or clarify anything about the massage, so I didn't even think to ask for a description of a "Sasakese massage," even though something told my husband to sit this one out.

It turns out that a Sasakese massage is the kind of thing you try once just to have had the experience, like the spicy Lombok chili pepper that gives the island its name, unless you're a masochist. That's not to say the massage therapist was a sadist, only that one must enjoy intense and prolonged pain to seek out this kind of massage. Seeing as I don't generally enjoy pain, I will never willfully get this massage again. But, I would be loath to say that I got nothing out of it. I must admit that the massage therapist did make me aware of parts of my body that I didn't know existed or could feel pain. That's worth something, I suppose.

I kissed my husband goodbye outside the small massage house where I went that fateful evening. It was modeled after a traditional Sasak fisherman's hut, except that this thatched-roof house had the modern addition of large picture windows on all walls. To the left of the entrance was a room with two raised massage beds, essentially the exact type of room I was expecting. However, I was not to enter that room. My room was to the right. My room, where I would be for the next ninety minutes, was entirely empty save for a single mattress on the floor covered by a colorful sheet, positioned directly below a long wooden bar that ran lengthwise, four feet above the mattress.

My massage therapist, an older Sasak man who told me later that his massage techniques had been passed down from his great-great-grandfather, asked me to lay on the mattress face down. He covered me with the sheet, and from the very first touch, I couldn't stop thinking over and over in my head that my husband would not like this massage. I uttered various iterations of this idea obsessively in my mind for the first half hour as the massage therapist used his knees and heels to jab, poke, and slide across my back.

The first thirty minutes turned out to be the warm-up, the Sasak version of a gentle back rub. The real massage started when he began running his strong fingers up and down the veins of my legs. That wasn't so bad, at first. It tickled when he got particularly high on my thigh or when he squeezed the jiggly bits of my leg, but the pain really began in earnest when he started pinching deep into my legs and drawing his thumb across my veins in rapid succession.

All the movements were performed methodically, beginning with my right calf. He worked his hand slowly up as he jabbed his thumb deep in the area that sometimes causes me to awake in the night with a charley horse, pitching his pointer finger and thumb across the veins inside. No matter my cries, he continued. Next, his hands made their way up to my right thigh, his fingers still unrelentingly focused on the veins deep inside my leg where I have never dared poke so deeply.

He massaged—for a lack of a better word—one leg at a time, so it felt slightly torturous knowing that my left leg awaited the same treatment. The time it took him to move across the mattress from one leg to the other felt excruciatingly long, the anticipation of pain worse than the actual pain of the massage. I'm kidding. The actual massage was way worse pain than I could have ever conjured up. Never in my life have I been so grateful to have only one back, one neck and one head where his methods could only be performed once.

When he moved on to my feet, he pressed hard onto the flat area on the outside of my foot by my ankle, which caused me to cry out in pain. Then he pressed into the arch and scraped his thumb across the veins on top of my foot. It's difficult to explain this whole scraping act because it is so unlike any pain or feeling I have ever had in my life. The top of the foot is not usually a place that engages with the outside world, except with the inside of shoes. It is normally free from pain unless it is stepped on, but even a wayward high heel is less painful than a Hulk-like thumb deliberately drawing itself across the veins that lie between bone and skin.

After the legs, he asked me to sit up and I did so facing the windows of the front wall. My massage took place between the hours of five and six thirty so I could tell the passing of time by the line of the setting sun on the mountain across the way. Every inch higher meant a moment closer to putting on my clothes and walking back to my husband, my gentle, gentle husband who would soon be tasked with giving me a massage to counteract this massage. I could hear some birds singing above me, sitting under the thatched roof, and I couldn't help but think that they were commiserating with me, acknowledging the predicament we both found ourselves in, both of us trapped in a place we had willfully come.

When I was seated, crisscross applesauce, the massage therapist proceeded to hang from the poll above us and press against my back with his feet. He placed each of my arms through his arms so that they dangled like a scarecrow's. Next, leaning back with his body still hanging by the pole, he wrapped his legs around me and pressed his feet into my bent knees to hold them in place. The final movement was one graceful and swift twist that caused my entire back to crack effortlessly.

When we untangled from that maneuver, it was time for my arms. He used the same deep scraping technique up and down my arms that he had used on my legs, only this time he ended at my elbow and pressed on a point under the bone so forcefully that I lost feeling in my hands. It was at this point—after some whimpering and involuntary spasms from the pain—that he asked if everything was okay, more than an hour into the massage. I said that it hurt a lot, and I couldn't help but laugh and squirm sometimes when it tickled. He said that many people disliked this massage. I asked if it was because it hurt them, and he said, yes, many people cry.

I'll admit that this made me feel a little better about the quiet murmurings of pain that I had allowed myself to produce, and I felt even proud that I was nowhere near tears. I looped back to my original thought that if my husband had managed to sit through the massage this long he would have been in tears, no doubt.

After this interaction, the massage therapist asked me to lay down on my back. If the arms were the most painful part of the massage, then this next part on my back was absolutely the most bizarre. He began with a series of stretches that reminded me of a physical therapy session. He pressed my straightened legs down toward my torso at different angles until they were open in the butterfly position. I'm flexible by nature so I had no problem with this part, but I can imagine that it would probably be an extremely painful portion of the massage for less flexible people.

The massage therapist seemed to give up on stretching my hips quickly after finding that he couldn't press my knees any further into the ground, so he straightened my legs out completely. Maybe if I hadn't been so flexible we never would have made it to this next part. Maybe if flights to South Korea had been less expensive, I would have been there, on a raised massage table, instead of here on the floor. Maybe if, maybe if.

In any case, we had time; the sun still cast a pink line of light on the mountain. He stood over me, slipped his hands under the small of my back and whispered what seemed like an incantation—though it was more likely a jumble of Sasakese curse words—before he picked me up by my back in one fell swoop and caught my hips in between his legs, the knobs of his knees managing to hold up the weight of my entire body as I hung there limp as a doll.

Holding me in this position, which I could see through my squinted eyes took a lot of effort on his part, he pressed his fingers into my collarbone and the muscles beneath it. I couldn't help but laugh a bit from the tickling. It felt disrespectful to be giggling while suspended in air by a man exerting so much energy on my behalf, but I kept my eyes closed, so maybe he didn't notice.

The final part of the massage was my head. The massage therapist pressed into my scalp with his palms and soon made his way to my face, sliding his hands across my forehead and temples. He pressed my ears inward and rubbed them, and I suddenly wondered in horror if he would massage my eyes. I think it's clear where this is going.

He put his hands on my face like he was blindfolding me, and pressed down, rippling his fingers several dozen times over my eyeballs. In this position, it was possible to appreciate the full strength of his hands, and it was the first time in my life that I really understood that someone could kill another human being by suffocating them with only their hands. I could never have pried his hands off my face, and I do believe he could have crushed any bone in my body. After a few minutes of the face massage and a few intense scratches on my head, he said the massage was over. Just like that, it was over.

There was still a tiny bit of light left in the sky, so I knew it must be a bit before the sunset at six thirty. I asked the massage therapist if I could take a shower in the bathroom, but to my surprise, he told me no. He said that I needed to wait thirty minutes. I asked him why and he said something that I didn't understand and the word red. It was something like, you have to wait for the red to stop. I guess he was referring to my blood, which had just been jostled every which way, so I got up and left.

I assume I was supposed to sit there and relax, but at that moment, the last thing I wanted to do was stay in the same room where everything had just gone down. I got up and put my clothes back on, still wet from an encounter with a giant wave on my way to the massage, and I remembered an earlier time, a world where I didn't know that the inside of my arms and legs felt pain, a world that no longer existed.

# WHAT DO MARES EAT?
Rob Dinsmoor

As I sat there in the surgeon's chair, with pieces of my skull removed around the temples, I had a moment to reflect on exactly how I wound up in this position. I was actually happy to be here. In the last few months, there had been times when I wanted to tear open my skull myself.

Try as I might, I hadn't been able to get rid of the tune out of my head. It crept into my consciousness slowly, insidiously, and I couldn't tell exactly when it started. I began humming it, at first, and then added some syllables: "Bo-Pe-Dope and Bo-Pe Dope and Dum-dum-dum ta dada . . ." It became so ingrained into my everyday thinking that I desperately wanted to identify its source. Was it a Top 40 song? Elevator music from somewhere I went frequently? An annoying TV jingle for some kids' cereal? A movie theme? A cell phone app?

Others noticed it even before I did. When I was at the library, the librarian looked over at me and put her finger to her lips before I was even aware of making any sound. A couple of times at work, someone peered over the wall of the cubicle and asked me to keep it down.

The tune began keeping me awake at night. And it was getting louder—in fact, sometimes it was so loud, I couldn't really hear myself think. It got in the way of my writing.

I mentioned it to my primary care doctor. "Does it distress you at all?" she asked.

"Well, yeah!" I said, and she referred me to a psychiatrist.

When I told my psychiatrist about it, he shrugged and said, "I've never encountered that problem before, but I'll bet some Zoloft would do the trick. It's a selective serotonin reuptake inhibitor. It's an antidepressant, but it's used for obsessive-compulsive disorder as well, so it might just work in this case."

I took the Zoloft religiously for nearly two months. When I came back for a follow-up visit, I told him that things hadn't really gotten any better. In fact, if anything, things had gotten worse: The tune had gotten louder and I found myself moving to its cadence. He went ahead and ordered me a "cocktail" of drugs, including a second SSRI called Wellbutrin and a different kind of medication, a tricyclic antidepressant known as amitriptyline. When that didn't work, he added risperidone, explaining that it was an antipsychotic.

"Are you saying I'm crazy?" I asked.

"Not at all," he said. "We use it in Tourette's syndrome, which is characterized by muscle tics, and it might just do the job in this case."

None of these things worked. Furthermore, they caused me to salivate and seemed to make my finer motor skills a little off. It was considerably harder to type, as my fingers tended to hit the wrong keys almost as often as they hit the right ones. And, meanwhile, the tune in my head got worse. It was no longer on the edge of my conscious. It was smack dab in the middle now, and what once was background music was now a loud, blaring brass band. I couldn't concentrate on anything and constantly found myself holding my ears, for all the good it did. I sometimes got drunk just to tune out the sound, and I woke up one morning with a terrible hangover, asking myself, "What kind of life is this?"

When I told my psychiatrist all this, he rubbed his eyes and said, "There's another tool in my armamentarium, but I'm reluctant to use it. Do you think you're at risk for suicide?"

"Well, I'm pretty distraught, but I wouldn't say—"

"Just say yes—" he prompted, and I did. "I'm going to recommend electroconvulsive shock therapy. Now, it's not as bad as it sounds. We sedate you and anesthetize you first, and you'll just go to sleep and wake up again—ideally, without the tune in your head."

They had me put on a hospital johnny and lie down on one of those reclining tables with one of those easily removable folding sheets. The technicians placed a rubber bite guard in my mouth, put conductive gel on my temples, and then placed electrodes on either side. I didn't notice any pain—I was just out. Unfortunately, when I awoke, the music was even louder than before. So loud, in fact, that the first thing I did when I came to was throw up all over my gown.

The psychiatrist called in a neurologist who, in turn, called in a neurosurgeon. They talked for a while in the corner and then came to me.

"It sounds as if you have some sort of micro-lesion in your auditory cortex," the neurosurgeon said. "Here's the game plan. We have to ablate—or destroy—that tiny portion of your brain where the tune is stored. What we'll do is stimulate various regions of your auditory cortex with electrodes until we find the exact spot that elicits the tune. And then, and only then, we'll destroy that tiny piece of tissue. You'll be awake, but it'll be completely painless because the scalp is anesthetized and the brain itself has no pain receptors."

They shaved my scalp, applied topical anesthesia, and gave me a sedative. I was transported to a sterile-looking blue room with extremely bright lights—like the light in a dentist's office, only much bigger. I got to watch the whole procedure on a small television monitor. They used a gizmo that looked like a portable fan to saw the top of my skull off. When they started stimulating things, I heard a host of different sounds: car horns, fireworks, bees buzzing, waterfalls. As disturbing as this sounds, it was a welcome relief from the tune. The sound was often accompanied by a faint vision or smell, and sometimes my fingers twitched.

After about an hour of this, I heard the tune. *Mares eat*

*oats and does eat oats and little lambs eat ivy…* It was "Mairzy Doats And Dozy Doats," a very silly little song I had heard as a kid. Over and over, in fact, because it was my favorite piece of music—a yellow 78 rpm record that my parents had given me for my fifth birthday and which I kept playing over and over again, much to my mother's chagrin.

"That's it! That's the tune!" I explained.

Suddenly, I was overcome with sadness. I was five years old, it was a summer evening back in our old Victorian Park Street house in Bloomington, Indiana, and a humid breeze was wafting through the open living room windows. I could smell Mom making spaghetti sauce—my favorite! I looked everywhere for my beloved 78, and finally found it—broken—under the couch. It was still in one piece but had a crack right down one side of it. Crying hysterically, I brought it over to my mother who was stirring the sauce and asked her to make it better.

"It can't be fixed!" she said. "I'm so sorry."

There was sympathy in her voice, but there was also something more. And now I realized what it was—guise. The broken record had been no accident!

"Great!" said the neurosurgeon, snapping me out of my reverie. "We've located the tune. Now it's just a matter of using an electrified hair-thin needle to thermally ablate the tissue."

She clamped some sort of guiding instrument to the side of my head and used it to insert the needle.

The tune faded from my head, as did the painful memory. I began to cry.

# A DAIHATSU DOCTOR
Roland Barnes

The thirty-yard slope, or *rampa*, to our house in the Alto Minho region of Portugal was laid centuries ago, with enormous lumps of granite worn smooth by human footwear, the cloven hooves of sheep and goats, oxen yoked to carts, and torrents of rainwater, which turned it into a stream during winter storms when the same boulders became indispensable as steppingstones. At one time, the giant cobbles may have provided a passable surface but, by our first ascent, they mostly resembled a random rock fall, some sunken deeply down and others rearing alarmingly up. When it was resurfaced with granite steps in 2006, the municipal engineer in charge told us it had been one of the diverse 15th-century pilgrim routes to the sacred site of Santiago de Compostela in northwest Spain. We liked the idea of owning a house with such visible signs of antiquity, but quickly realized the impossibility of driving an ordinary car up to the front door. The solution was a Daihatsu Rocky, marketed in Britain as a Fourtrak, heavy as a tank, but comfortable enough for the 2,400-mile return trip from home in southeast London through the Channel Tunnel via southwest France and northern Spain. Making such long journeys at high speeds probably caused the damage.

Another reason for buying a truck was Portugal's notoriously dangerous driving conditions. Today, the journey to our house from Francisco Sá Carneiro Airport—bizarrely named after a former Prime Minister who lost his life in an air crash—takes an hour along the A3 Motorway, a 21st-century highway we depart at Sapardos, before bypassing the 20th and negotiating twisting byways home. In 1995, on my first trip north in a tinny hire car, the shadowy coast road by Viana do Castelo was a speed track of recklessly driven goods vehicles and heedless saloon car drivers veering abruptly left to overtake, or inexplicably stopping dead in front of me during driving rain. On one narrow stretch, swerving onto a grass verge was the only way to avoid a pair of headlights coming directly at me on the wrong side of the carriageway. It happened so quickly, I instinctively rejoined the road and carried on, like a Scalextric car suddenly righting itself after going off the track. The next stretch, inland over narrow mountain roads with visibility reduced to a few feet by a combination of darkness and swirling mist, was hair-raising. I was lucky to get there in one piece.

One summer, I was driving my wife down the A3 to the airport when the gearbox jammed in fourth. Luckily, we were close to Barcelos services, able to pull in and think about what to do next. In a hurry to catch a plane, Diane phoned for a taxi, which screeched into the car park where she was already positioned to jump in. In my case, it was a matter of limping thirty miles along country lanes to the garage of Carlos Duarte da Silva Capucho in our village. We'd met already one frosty morning when he came out with jumper cables to get me started. Perhaps anticipating future business, he wouldn't accept payment but, whatever his motives, his laconic style was impressive. A damaged gearbox was a much bigger proposition than a flat battery, as locating Daihatsu parts in rural north Portugal was never going to be easy. The vehicle was stuck in Carlos's "*oficina*" or workshop for more than six weeks, the replacement parts eventually arriving in big cardboard boxes from Osaka via Madrid.

Such a wait meant regular long walks to the garage to monitor progress; feigning friendship with an ugly hound straining on a chain outside the entrance and being prepared to engage in bewildering conversations about the functions of gearbox parts with names barely recognizable even in

English. Many's the time my fractured Portuguese has led to *malentendidos*, or misunderstandings. Buying furniture in a gloomy emporium where the shopkeeper, in a black suit, white shirt, and plain tie, looked more like an undertaker, I used for wood the word *lenha* instead of the correct *madeira*, inquiring: "Can you please tell me what kind of firewood this bed is made of?" Negotiating with Carlos and his mechanic was another stiff test; interchanges ended abruptly with mutual head shaking and embarrassed handshakes.

Three years and 50,000 miles later, the overtaxed engine suffered a complete pressure failure warranting total reconditioning. Months of treatment meant another visit to the airport to hire a vehicle until new parts arrived from abroad. Seeing an assortment of engine parts lying disjointedly on the garage floor made me wonder whether reassembly was beyond even the power of Carlos Capucho. What would happen if he couldn't fix it? Was it worth shipping back to Britain or just leave it to rot? But there was no need to worry. For much of his working life, he'd been a Formula One mechanic at the *Autódromo do Estoril*, home of the Portuguese Grand Prix between 1984-1996, knowing all there was to know about car engines, even alien Daihatsus. One afternoon, a familiar horn tone at the bottom of our lumpy lane announced we were on the road again.

Having spent most of his life in Lisbon, Carlos was scathing about the villagers in his birthplace. In turn, they scorned his services, seeking cheaper alternatives from repairers with fewer credentials in neighboring villages, but there was a nucleus of discerning regulars to keep him in business. I was careful to avoid taking the jeep in for servicing on Mondays if his football team, Benfica, had gone down that weekend. Always quick with a joke, his serious conversations were generally underpinned by wry humor, but he was also an ardent "Eagles" fan and, if his team had lost, it was difficult to get a civil word out of him. It's something football fans everywhere have in common, but it's worse for the Portuguese who are an emotional lot. In the absence of something really dramatic—a tragic air crash or terrorist attack—coverage of games takes pride of place as first feature on evening television, relegating what might appear to the neutral observer to be more important political matters to the tail end of news bulletins. At an international level, Portuguese victories produce outbursts of media orchestrated xenophobia, whilst defeat brings tears as the whole country goes into mourning.

His one mechanic was nearing retirement; he and the boss were often seen climbing out of an inspection pit covered from head to toe in oil and grease. It was the kind of workshop depicted in French and Italian neo-realist films from the 1940s, walls decorated with smeared Valvoline posters advertising motor rallies where the finishing line had been crossed many years earlier. When he was not down there or underneath a bonnet, Carlos sat behind his cluttered desk in a cubby-hole with oily fingerprints on every surface. A cigarette always on the go, he peered at me quizzically over spectacles perched on the end of his nose as he totted up the bill. Calculation complete, he stretched his arms out wide in mock apology when presenting me with the final figure: "*Muito caro*" (meaning very expensive), he explained in his tarry voice, raising his eyes skyward as though fixing the price was in the hands of a supernatural force beyond his control. When he passed it over for me to scrutinize, it became my turn to dolefully shake my head in a parody of amazed disbelief, knowing all too well it would soon be time to cough up. Despite top prices, Carlos kept us on the road for a decade, always willing do minor repairs without charging a penny.

With the vehicle now in good repair, it was some time before I noticed the guard dog gone and the heavy double doors locked and bolted. On the upper-story of the same building used to be a small supermarket recently moved to another part of the village. Early in 2015, I asked the shopkeeper, who knew him well, how Carlos was getting on, and he told me he'd died from lung cancer the previous year; chain-smoking in a perpetual haze of oil and petrol fumes was not conducive to long life.

At the ripe old age of twenty, with 135,000 miles on the clock, the jeep, now based in Wales, is not in the best of health either. Although the engine is as smooth as it was when Carlos rebuilt it, the gearbox suddenly began knocking in third. My first thought was it was time for the junkyard, but discarding it felt like being disrespectful to the man who'd put so much skill and effort into keeping it going. So, a reconditioned box has been fitted, a new starter motor is in place, rusty sills repaired, and bodywork touched up. It's not what you would call "good as new" but, as we are now reliant on train and plane to the Alto Minho, Rocky's only going as far as the supermarket.

# THE TAXI I CALLED
Saundra Norton

The Taxi I Called
never showed up.
I called again.
A voice informed me
I had already been picked up,
but they could send another
if I needed to go again.
I noticed a single lavender stiletto heel
on the floor of my room.
My suitcase already bulging
I heard the taxi horn.
Clutching the shoe,
I raced outside and down the street,
three blocks before he stopped.
The driver leaned out the window
to ask me directions,
not realizing it was me
he was trying to find,
chasing him, waving a lavender shoe.
We were almost to the airport
when, over the radio,
I heard my address being read.
The driver turned and said,
*I will ignore him and take you instead.*

# JAPANESE TAXIS AND ELEMENTARY INCIDENTS

Anthony Head

We were stuck in traffic on the Bayswater Road when my cabby struck up conversation. On learning that I live in Tokyo he inquired what the taxis are like in Japan. I gave some lazily equivocal reply that underscored London's status as taxi heaven. But it was one of those questions that tempt the response, "How much time do you have?" And it sent my mind fumbling back across the years in recollection.

During my early days in Japan there were few things I enjoyed more than a taxi ride. An alien in an alien land, I had relished the sense of adventure in being ferried at night through unknown city streets, their neon lights ablaze, or by day through mosaics of urban paddy fields toward some distant temple. To plunge into warmth from the biting winter winds or find air-conditioned sanctuary from the blistering summer heat was a kind of bliss that bordered on the transcendent.

Many years and several thousand journeys later, I often find familiarity has bred something akin to its usual offspring. Like many foreigners, I have run the gamut of Japanese taxi experience, from the banal to the bizarre, the vivifying to the terrifying, and in a land where even in recent years an annual traffic death toll of 10,000 was par for the course, still to be alive is itself no mean achievement. Especially have I had my fill of late-night taxi rides home from the office—the speeding and tailgating on the narrow, elevated expressways that snake through central Tokyo out into the suburbs, my pleas with the drivers to slow down or keep their distance, or the hours spent inching forward past lanes blocked off because of a collision, often involving a taxi. It was the trauma of March 2011 that persuaded me not to travel on an elevated expressway again, the last place, apart from a deep subway train, I would want to be trapped when the next big earthquake strikes. (Still in my mind is the revelation that when the Hanshin Expressway toppled over during the huge Kobe quake in 1995, plastic bottles, sweet wrappers, paper bags and whatnot were among the discovered items that workers had idly thrown into the concrete mix for the support columns.)

My first ride in a Japanese taxi set the pattern for many another, ending up where I didn't want to go. A novice English teacher fresh off the plane, I had hailed a cab after my first sortie into the nighttime wonderland of Tokyo. The Dai-Ichi Hotel was my destination, the driver duly delivered me, and it was only then I discovered there was one in Ginza as well as Shimbashi. But two things I took for granted then came to impress me later: the driver knew the way, and he had stopped to pick me up. Japan is a country where the cities have few street names and many taxi journeys are completed on foot, from the drop-off point of a railway station or landmark building. "The Knowledge" of the London cabby has no equivalent here, and it was often the case that without a detailed road map a driver would get lost. I had drivers stop to ask the way of other drivers, or get out to inquire for directions at police stations. Some I managed to put out of their misery through sudden recognition of my surroundings or simple lucky guesses; others I sometimes, when all hope was gone, abandoned mid-journey to chance my luck with another.

The advent of satellite navigators has largely consigned such experiences to the past (though their curiously double function as television sets does little to settle the nerves when the driver has half an eye on some Yomiuri Giants' slugfest). Yet, even now, cabbies who know the destination—or can easily find it on the screen—often ask which route the customer wishes to take. In the days before Sat Navs, a noncommittal response would often induce confusion or discomfort. One extreme manifestation was a young driver so nervous that his hands were shaking on the wheel as I climbed into the back seat. Straightaway, he turned to me and pleaded for directions, and the terror in his eyes would have been no less had I been the Emperor himself: it was his first day on the job, he didn't know Tokyo at all, he didn't know if he would last the day…

I was able to guide him street by street and he began to talk about himself. He had come from Fukui Prefecture, fleeing the provincial life where only fishing and the nuclear power plants offered any hope of work. But would he ever know the city? He had seen it on television but didn't think it would be like this. I tried to encourage him with tales of less legitimate ignorance, if failing to resist some portentous brag about the London cabby's knowledge, and when, our destination reached, I waved away the balance, I had to reassure him that this, too, was all in order. There might be no tipping in Japan, but I'd never met a taxi driver who wasn't pleased to keep the change.

But most of all, in seeking to allay his paranoia with a revelation of my own, I had thanked him for stopping to pick me up at all. There are few sights more deflating to the spirit, or provoking to the humors, of the foreign resident in Japan than the rear end of a taxi that, having slowed to all but a standstill, suddenly speeds away at the whim of the demon behind the wheel. The late Alan Booth, in one of his columns for an English-language daily, once suggested a curative for these bouts of high blood pressure in the form of a sprint in pursuit of the offending vehicle and the hefty application to its rear end of a sturdy walking boot—advice which drew dissenting response on the Letters page from more than one straight-faced reader.

I have often heard this tendency ascribed, by Japanese friends and strangers alike, to a simple lack of English on the driver's part—not a willful discrimination, but a harmlessly more human one, a last-minute loss of nerve to avoid exposure as a failed linguist. Nonetheless, only in Japan have I had to hide behind a hedge in order to catch a cab.

An English colleague and I had been drinking on a wet Friday night, like half the population of Tokyo it seemed, and the taxis were circling, taking their pick of the custom caught on the glistening streets. Possibly my attire didn't help, though jeans and leather jacket are not usually an impediment. Perhaps I needed a haircut or a shave. My colleague intimated as much after several slowing taxis had shown us their rear ends, immaculately groomed as he was in stockbroker's suit and Burberry. So, the ploy was hatched: I would disappear behind a nearby hedge and my colleague, with briefcase raised to shield his lowered head, would lure the prey with the promise of a corporate expense account. Sure enough, within a minute I had got the call, hurdled the hedge, and projected myself into the back of the car before the astonished driver could reach for the lever to shut the door.

From that moment onward, I found a briefcase the most valuable accessory for the foreign taxi hunter. Whether to shield the face from direct view, or simply to suggest respectability, the possession of a briefcase invariably brings results, and, on many nights, I would venture out onto the town with an empty case in hand.

But now with *omotenashi* being the new buzzword in Japan, I doubt that the thousands flocking to Tokyo for the 2020 Olympics will have cause to resort to such tactics while enjoying the "wholehearted hospitality" on offer. First-timers should beware, though, of the Japanese taxi's most distinctive feature. Remote-controlled doors have undoubted advantages for customers making a headlong entrance from a hedge, but peril awaits those who take their eyes off them for a moment, as I once did on a warm spring evening in Kyoto, not long after my arrival.

I had been to a concert with four young ladies from the company I worked for, all of whom had inspired in me fantasies of lust reciprocated. We were having no luck in finding a cab, and I had moved up the road by myself. Shortly, an approaching taxi slowed and, to my astonishment, pulled up beside me. As I called back in triumph to my companions, the door swung open and, with the unleashed force of its own momentum, caught me where my airy cotton trousers offered scant protection. The *sensei* crumpled, aware in his writhing only of a few scattered cherry blossoms on the pavement fading out of focus as the water welled in his eyes. His recollection of that evening ends there, with the voices of four figures standing over him, chattering, consoling, giggling, and he was never to succeed in inspiring amorous inclinations in any of the objects of his desire.

But once such barriers to admittance have been overcome, it's inside the taxi that aspects of the true Japanese sub-culture reveal themselves. And for the driver anxious to break the ice with his solitary foreign customer, what better subject for discussion indeed than amorous inclinations? One, with the punch perm suggestive of his underworld connections, initiated this topic not by speech but by holding up a gold-encrusted hand and waggling his little finger. When he saw my comprehending smile, his inquiring glance in the rear-view mirror softened and dialogue commenced. How was it going with Japanese women? Was I scoring? More importantly, was I scoring enough? And while we were on the topic, what was my favorite position? What? Foreigners liked that too? Hehhhhh! And what about Soapland? Well, I should go. I knew the massage parlors in Thailand, of course, but the Japanese ones were better...

Thus, we passed a pleasant twenty minutes, in which Japanese women became Japanese woman, the commodity on display in the daily sports papers and late-night television shows and ubiquitous mailbox leaflets. Perhaps it was from this very taxi that I pulled from one of the pouches on the seatback—mostly filled with flyers for mobile phones or golf club memberships—a brochure advertising Office Ladies, or "Love Call from Charming OLs" as the cover has it. Inside, a leggy woman in leather and silk perches on the edge of a billiards table, her skirt riding up as she lines up her cue beneath the English slogan: "I will take your phone message." Another, in a see-through skirt, bends down to open a limousine door, her underwear outlined beneath the motto: "I would like be your secretary."

Standard discourse, though, tends to a different pattern: the customer's Japanese is excellent (this after "Shinjuku Station, please")—is the customer American? So, where is the customer from? How long has the customer been in Japan? Can the customer eat Japanese food? There follows a series not so much of inquiries as assertions seeking confirmation. What the equivalent for passengers from Italy or Australia or Sweden might be, I can only guess, and guess well enough. But I could never compute the times I've been told that mine is the land of the "English gentleman," that London is foggy, that my countrymen always carry umbrellas, and that I drink tea not coffee. And whether I indulge with jovial assent, or evoke the football hooligan, or observe that the city of Sherlock Holmes is a century past, or note that annual rainfall in Japan is greater than in Britain, is often determined by nothing more definable than the driver's tone of voice. Once, I had a driver who, on learning my nationality, replied reassuringly, "England, I know"—and proceeded to punctuate the rest of the journey with exclamatory interrogatives: "Aaah, Victoria!" "Yes." "Aaah, Churchill!" "Yes." "Aaah, Thatcher!" "Yes." It seemed an age until I could clamber out, but finally, the door slammed shut and the taxi sped away, the syllables "Bobby Charlton!" hanging in the midnight air.

But it's naturally the departures from the pattern that stick in the mind, like the driver who talked nostalgically of Norwich, choking with emotion as he struggled to express the intangible importance this old cathedral city had assumed in his private mythology. A three-month homestay in the only place on the planet he had ever been outside Japan had become the very symbol of carefree life, and in his dreams of future happiness, all roads led back to East Anglia. Or the driver who wanted me to sing. This was long before the *karaoke* boom took off overseas and in the days when foreigners were scarce, even in the suburbs of monstrous Osaka where I was living at the time. But he had his mini tape deck all set up and laughed aside my attempts to demur. Mercifully, the tape became entangled in its spool, sparing me the pains of "Yesterday," but he passed me the microphone anyway, its cord getting wrapped around the gear stick, and said I must sing something else. No music. Just sing. It was a scorching day. Outside, the sun beat down on scattered figures in the fields, bent double under wide-brimmed hats, and as we bumped along the ditch-lined roads, the crickets and cicadas rasping in the grasses, a bullet train thundered by in the distance, and in hopeless imitation of my beloved Mel Tormé, I sang "Blue Moon" to my audience of one.

As taxis are the only form of public transport that enable passengers routinely to engage with their drivers, perhaps it's not surprising that even ten minutes in their company can leave such indelible impressions. A moment's recollection and I can call up a gallery of characters to the forefront of my mind, knowing nothing of them other than a word or gesture or expression. There was the driver with the dyed curly hair, silent throughout a slow journey on a humid afternoon, who suddenly walked off in the middle of a traffic jam, returning a few minutes later with two cans of cold coffee from a vending machine and wordlessly tossing one to me in the back seat.

There was the big, bald driver who talked incessantly of heaven knows what, encouraged by the grunts and gurgles I employ when I need to veil my ignorance to keep the conversation flowing, and who, turning, at last, to hand me my change, literally shrieked, his eyes all but bursting from their sockets, at the sight of a foreign face, so perfect had been my Japanese. There was the wiry, bird-like driver who, one freezing winter's night when the snow lay thick over Tokyo, ferried me home at ten miles an hour through roads packed high with ice and dotted with abandoned cars, and who laughed whenever the taxi slithered out of control a strange and high-pitched cackle which blended the exuberance of childish delight with that of maniacal intent.

And there was the driver I wanted to throttle. He watched impassively from behind the wheel, his face veiled in smoke, while I struggled in the rain to remove a motorbike and its drunken rider collapsed in the middle of a narrow side street. We had stopped a few meters short of the heap and he had muttered to himself in irritation, before leaning back and lighting a cigarette. The black leather figure wrapped around the bike was a hefty young woman, ungrazed but half asleep, as heavy as several sacks of potatoes. Somehow, I managed to drag her to the roadside and get her to her feet, holding her face up to the rain. She came to and seemed to recognize her surroundings. She claimed to live nearby and I made her promise to walk the rest of the way, for all the good that may have done. I returned to the taxi, drenched and exhausted. "Drunk, I suppose," was the driver's only comment. He had kept the meter running and, by the time I reached home, the fare was twice the usual sum. I was too tired to remonstrate or to thank him for his help. But since this is Japan, where "case by case" is the nation's favorite adage, there was also not long afterward the clean-cut driver with the manicured fingernails, insistently pressing a refund on me since the roadwork on the shortest route had forced us into a detour.

And it's not unusual to find these extremes in closer combination. Only recently, after waiting aeons in the early hours of a Saturday morning, I spotted a taxi trapped by traffic lights at a nearby crossing. I raised my hand to the driver as I approached, and felt, at once, as his face didn't flicker, that familiar blend of helpless resignation and impotent rage. I stood by the door and waited for it to open. I tapped on the window. I lowered my head to the driver's level. I called out politely. But nothing altered his expressionless features or the fixed direction of his stare. I had stumbled across a master of *mokusatsu*, the time-honored Japanese method of killing one's enemy with silence. I doubt that even a briefcase would have given me a semblance of identity.

The lights changed and he shot off at speed, breaking heavily thirty meters down the road to pick up a young Japanese couple. For a moment, I contemplated the Booth solution, but knew my shoes weren't up to it. Scarcely had I bawled some choice invective into the night air than another taxi pulled up and the door swung open. The driver chatted politely all the way home, a model of affability, while the sound of birdsong and the gentle trickle of a mountain stream filtered through from two small speakers behind the rear seat. A sticker on the door beside me, thoughtfully translated into English, read: "Fasten seat belt. Prepare for accident." I would have, had the belt-clip not been lost in the crevice of the seat. Strangely reassured, I forbore to mention the Clean Air Acts as the driver held forth on foggy London and Sherlock Holmes.

# SELF-PORTRAIT
Richard Luftig

He has been to most
of the wonders of the world;
Grand Canyon, Eifel Tower,
The Great Wall, and seen

none, his back to them all.
Here at the Islands,
in shorts, Hawaiian shirt
and a lei, and this one

on top of a gorge at Yosemite,
out on a ledge in a cowboy hat
a jaunty look on his face,
flirting with death as he edges

ever back so his camera can get
a better view of the canyon
six-thousand feet below.
And not just places

but animals too: the panda
in the National Zoo,
tigers from Circus World,
Alligators at Swamp-O-Rama,

Even the herd of llamas
from the alpaca farm,

*me at Machu Picchu*
*me at the Pyramids*

all downloaded
somewhere he hopes
at least ten people
will give him a *like*.

And he never knowing
all he's missed unless
he shows up uninvited on
someone else's video.

# THE MAN WITH NO OUTLINES
Jain Tushar

At seven fifteen in the morning, the sun was soft in the sky. I've often woken as early as I can manage simply to watch the night sky turn violet first, as drops of daylight seep into the dark, spread, disturb its purity. But there's nothing quite like the hours that follow, when everything gets saturated, slowly, with a new day. In Mumbai, if you happen to live close to the sea, there's very little that can compare to watching night being harried out of a room by degrees. Its muggy warmth is upset, its color dispelled and its deep silence eroded bit by bit, by the unclasping of windows, birdsong, the creak of old bicycles, carrying a crisp sheaf of newspapers, trapped on the pillion.

That day, as per my new routine, I was out in the park, just beginning my rounds. The Colaba Sukh Sagar Park has a six hundred and forty meters long path that snakes through it. Almost every morning, the park is teeming with people. Trees, mostly banyans, surround you on either side. In the warmer months, the place is speckled with snow-white egrets. Varicolored, expectant cats wait at the entrance, mewling, their eyes widening as you pass them by. In the sprawling park, somewhere, I heard someone say there's a massive sundial.

That Tuesday, the crowd was scarce and scattered. Mid-August rains had dissuaded many from turning up. Those who had were careful not to run on the damp stone of the path. The usual smell of fish, which hangs in the air like an apparition, had grown prominent. The oldest park-goers, who were also the source of the loud, daily exhalations of "Om," were missing. I could vaguely guess why. Monsoons, my late grandfather used to say, turned him into a creaking chair, his bones into a thing of music.

I had barely begun with my walk, covered some fifty meters when I noticed him sitting there.

Of course, I had seen him before. Twice, to be exact. Once, I'd seen him standing outside a store, lost in thought, maybe trying to make up his mind if he should enter. And another time, I had seen him from across the street, stooping, offering food to a cat. I couldn't make out what it was, but the cat, raggedy, evil-looking, didn't seem to enjoy it very much. It stalked away, the gobbet of food untouched, scarcely a moment or two before I did.

At the moment, he was sitting by himself on a park bench. The mellow, sweet flavor of the weather didn't seem to have affected him in the least. He was glumly staring at his feet. He didn't look happy about the entrancing color the sky had taken up, about the fact that we'd beaten the sun and rain to the park or about the dull but pleasant beat of life all around us.

Let me be clear. I am not some peppy extrovert. Far from it. I like being left alone, at times, and can empathize when someone desires a bit of solitude too. But the man on the bench didn't fit the description of someone who wanted to be alone. And because I had heard of people like him, I knew that that was the last thing he could possibly want. And so, it was nothing but sympathy that drove me to upset my routine and approach him instead.

"Hello," I said, walking over to him. He looked up.

*Hello.*

"Okay if I sit here?"

*Sure*, he said. It was difficult to make out his tone. I'd heard that it takes a little while to get used to their way of talking. And it was my very first time meeting a Man With No Outlines.

*Can you see that? The bird?* he asked, all of a sudden, pointing at something.

At first, I couldn't make out what it was he was indicating.

Squinting, I finally did. It was amazing that he could see that far without any difficulty. Perhaps, I guessed, eyes that lacked specific shape and form, that were merely colors floating on a face, tended to be sharper than the ordinary pair. Maybe it was the one good thing about being who he was.

He had spotted a sparrow close to where the path started. From this distance, I would've been unable to spot it, if the people who entered the park didn't keep stopping to look at it. Also, what helped greatly was the way it was thrashing about.

The sparrow was near the twisting roots of a banyan, one of many. Somehow, it had been caught badly in a riot of black thread. I decided, a second later, that it probably wasn't some ordinary black thread but bitingly sharp kite string. Which made sense too. With the Independence Day having just gone by, the sky had been dotted with soaring, dipping orange, green and tri-colored kites. The poor bird must've had the misfortune, I imagined, of getting caught in a spare length of cut string left hanging from the old, shaggy banyan looming over it.

I could understand why the passersby chose to keep away from the sparrow. I, too, wouldn't have been persuaded to set it free. The bird was putting up an enormous struggle. It was pecking mightily at the strings, fighting for its freedom, rolling to and fro on the wet grass. Even from where I sat, it was an impressive sight. It was also quite obvious that any thoughtful human hands that reached for the thrashing, determined sparrow would come away pecked, mercilessly, and bleeding.

*I think I can help it*, the Man With No Outlines said, distracting my attention.

"You can? So...what's stopping you?"

The man looked at me. It was a sad, piteous look. I realized a little late that I had asked a very stupid question.

"I'm sorry. I didn't mean—"

*No, no, no, it's okay*, he said.

I felt worse now. I had begun to understand his tone. He had brushed off my apology quickly, almost eagerly. He didn't wish to upset me. He needed me to be next to him. His desperation, his loneliness was painfully palpable. While I wanted to keep sitting there, for his sake, I simultaneously had begun to feel that it might've been a mistake coming over. I should have kept walking, done my rounds, gone home.

*What do you do?*

Again, this took me by surprise. He hadn't told me his name or asked for mine. You exchanged names, perhaps talked about trifling things like the weather or the news, fostered some familiarity, and only then, I've come to learn, shifted to more personal topics. I had always thought that that was the order of all exchanges with a stranger. This novel approach made me somewhat uneasy.

"I...I'm a mathematician."

I did not want to blurt this out. Had the conversation been more routine, I would've come up with a clever lie. But he had caught me off-guard and I spat out the truth. I grew worried that I'd made another terrible faux pas, accidentally humiliated him again. Thankfully, he chortled.

*That's funny*, he said, grinning widely.

I felt relieved that he thought so. In my career, I've come to realize that *Mathematics* is a strong, suggestive word. It conjures an image the moment it's spoken. Images that always connote the same things—decisiveness, form, structure, an endless array of lines, straight or curving, as if bent on a knee. Basically, everything he grotesquely lacked. I didn't think for a second that the stark irony of the both of us sitting on that bench offered a choice, could be anything but hurtful. Apparently, it could be. It could be amusing.

*My wife's leaving me.*

Another non-sequitur from him! I've had a lot of time to think about that bizarre un-conversation. There was no civilized flow to the way we talked that day. Flouting conventions so brazenly, I felt immensely self-aware that I was doing something wrong and desperately wished for it to stop. If only we weren't being such adventurers, if only he would tell me his name, ask for mine in turn. Since then, I've had ample time to put together why he talked the way he did. The reasons, as they emerged, were quite uncomplicated really. He had been alone for so long that he'd forgotten how to talk to strangers. For all I know now, he might've been doing his very best to sound "normal." But these realizations are a result of *years* of idle contemplation and hindsight. Right then, I just considered all of it unnatural and a bit odd.

"I'm sorry to hear that," I said honestly.

He shook his head. *I cannot blame her. I'm grateful that she stayed as long as she did. She's my dearest, my only friend. Was. I think that's why she stayed as long as she did. Not because she was my wife, but because she was my friend.*

I saw an opportunity to rein in this wild conversation here and took it before he could surprise me again.

"If she already knew she'd leave you eventually, why did she marry you?"

*We married long before...long before all of this...*

"Oh. I thought—"

*That's what everybody thinks at first,* he said, nodding. All the colors on his face moved, seeped into each other, blended with one another to form new, garish shades. *But no. I wasn't born this way. None of us are. I used to have a chemist shop in Worli. Years ago. I loved having a daily schedule, a waking time, a time to sleep, to eat, of going to work. All of that is gone.*

"So, when did it—"

*Happen?* he finished, eager to talk, to unburden an old load. *I—I cannot remember "everything." But I have these— these distinct memories of being a happy, organized man. I was the kind of person who would stop to admire a desk or a chair for its purposefulness. I had a fascination for old things, especially radios. The more clunky and broken and the more knobs missing, the better! My wife and I, we had a decent life together and we cherished it thoroughly. Kyurvi, my wife, taught Geography in a school, back then, to grades four and five. That might not seem like much to you, a mathematician, but she suffers from a terrible lisp. She had to give it her all to get that job. Both of us, we worked hard, didn't have much money, but we had the basic things we needed, and that felt more than enough. We felt blessed.*

"That sounds good," I said.

*It was,* he said. *Our very own little paradise.*

"So, again, I don't understand. What happened?"

The Man With No Outlines remained quiet for a beat. Then he spoke more quietly than before. Even though I had grown accustomed to his manner of talking by now, this time I had to strain to listen.

*It happened one day. I had drawn the shutter down on the shop and was waiting at the bus stop. I had closed up early and would have to wait some fifty minutes for the bus that took me from Worli to my flat in Thane. I cannot tell you where or how the thought entered my mind, but as I stood, waiting, at some point something hit me with great force. It was Doubt. It came out of nowhere. I wish there was some dramatic episode, some epiphany, you know, that brought it on. There wasn't. I was standing at a normal bus stop. And it—it found me.*

"Doubt?"

The Man With No Outlines nodded slowly, grimly.

*I went home puzzled and told myself that things would be better the next day. They weren't. They got worse. Kyurvi, my wife, noticed on the third day. My employees at the shop on the fourth. On the fifth day, two of the three didn't turn up for work. As superstitious as they were, they didn't even return to collect their salaries.*

As he kept talking, I felt a new, utterly unfamiliar disquiet, almost a panic, start to creep up on me. He'd said something that truly frightened me and sent a quick chill down my back. The bit about Doubt. Constant Doubt was a state that had existed throughout my life. It lived in the back of my mind, buried deep under lists of chores, worries, hopes, more. As he spoke about it then, I felt things, weightless things, move, budge, rise in me. I was struck by an unknown terror.

*Once Doubt had a strong enough hold,* he carried on, *it started showing up all over me, changing me, by and by. My definiteness, my outlines began to disappear. And once they did, people, those closest to me, realized what was happening and immediately distanced themselves. Friends I'd grown up with refused to take my calls or even speak to me when I turned up at their door.*

I wanted him to stop talking. Right then. Just stop. I tried speaking. "I need to—" I muttered lowly, but he barreled on, airing what he'd kept bottled up for too long.

*Suddenly, I found simple things impossibly difficult. I had this—this ever-expanding uncertainty. About everything! Over time, my voice changed. People don't realize this, but a voice, its tone too has shape, an outline. My lips were the last to lose their form; they became this melting red mess you see. People started staring at me, just staring blankly, and they looked away the second I tried approaching them. I felt judged at all times. I still do. At all times.*

"I need to go. I'm sorry, but I need to go right now!" I finally said, shaken up, jumping to my feet.

I wish he'd created a scene right then. I would've deserved the humiliation. Something overwhelmingly dramatic. Clung, with building intensity, onto the one person in perhaps ages who'd shown him some kindness. But he kept silent and hung his head. That, as I stalked off urgently, selfishly, made me feel woeful and horrible inside. Regardless, I knew I needed to get away from him as soon as I could because everything he'd said had made complete sense to me. What was worse was that it had stirred something in me.

I had walked only a few steps from him when I felt the slightest pinch of something on my hand. I brought it up to see what it was. And when I did, all breath was knocked out of me, as if I'd taken a punch in the stomach.

The nail on the ring finger of my left hand was different. Its outlines had entirely vanished. Its colors were running, leaking into the skin of my finger. Fear, total and formidable, stilled my heart. It scurried in me like something from a trap. It was an unmistakable symptom. Of the inevitable things and time to come.

I'm not fanatical about my health. I had only taken to the morning walks at the behest of my family doctor. My knees, you see, had been giving me trouble of late. Pointing at my X-rays, Dr. Makhija explained that, eventually, I would have to get knee-replacement surgery, get new, artificial joints planted like seeds. To help me along, for the time being, he stuck a long needle into my knee—a procedure I wouldn't wish upon my worst enemy—and, grinning devilishly, drew out a syringe full of brown, murky, foul-smelling liquid. Then, when, shortly, relief flooded my legs and pried away the pain, he advised me on the walks. But he strictly warned me against running, as that could further damage both the ruined joint and its surrounding tissue.

When I saw the fingernail, and what all it implied, I spun back to the Man With No Outlines. However, he looked so miserable sitting there, so unreservedly wretched, any rage that had sparked in me against him flickered out instantly. I lingered there for only a few seconds longer. And then, ignoring all sound medical advice and the protests that rose from my knees seconds later, I ran.

The only desire that remained in me was to hasten home to my wife. To get under the bed sheets again and nudge awake a sluggish, drowsy Anuva. To ensure, at that early hour, that she still loved me. To lightly insist she say it out loud, repeat it a couple of times. And all that time, I would be holding my hand behind my back like a child with a secret, making sure she didn't see.

As I ran from the park, the few who still remained watched me, intrigued. I wasn't jogging, I was sprinting. Like something crazy. But even in that mad rush to get home, I didn't fail to notice the sparrow near the start of the winding path. The defiant thing had finally pecked itself free of the kite string.

As I tore past the gate and into the street, the sparrow rose up too, above me, beating its thin wings, its cry triumphant, joyous. A woman, her hair in plastic curlers, leaned out of her window, crossing her arms on the sill. People began to materialize in the street, gather near *sabzi-wallahs*, bark raucous laughter. School-bound children, lugging heavy bags, came pouring out of buildings. Soon, the strays grew unafraid to bark, to shatter what remained of the stillness.

# MUSICAL CHAIRS AT LAKSHMI LODGE
Olga Pavlinova Olenich

Lakshmi Lodge was once a brothel. This makes sense. The goddess Lakshmi is the goddess of wealth. No doubt the brothel-keepers did a roaring trade in their time. The Lakshmi has one of the best positions in Mahabalipuram. It faces the Bay of Bengal, and the upper rooms and restaurant have an exquisite view over the sea and the Shore Temple. A Dutchman who settled in the Lakshmi as a long-term resident is said to have planted the magnificent garden in which the lodge is situated. This green oasis sets the Lakshmi apart from the other places along this stretch.

The Lakshmi Boys, friendly as they seem, are not of India's finest. The Lakshmi Boys have been around. They spend the day "looking after" the place in a desultory sort of way. They run a few errands, water a plant or two, and generally loll about. Some of them seem to sleep all day. You come across them curled up on a balcony, stretched out under the staircase, huddled in a chair in what passes for an office. At night they are more alert, looking for an opportunity. They are waiting for some wealthy Western woman to take them on and then, hopefully, take them home to an easy life. In the former enterprise, I have no doubt they've had their successes.

The lodge is a romantic place with its restaurant under the stars, its lush garden, its private balconies and terraces. Any newly arrived girl might find the setting and a pair of flashing dark eyes hard to resist, especially after a drink or two. Sadly, The Lakshmi Boys are strictly nocturnal. In the light of day, they are somehow lacking magic and nobody feels like taking them home. On a particularly enchanted evening (the moon was full, the stars were bright, the air was thick with the smell of the sea) my traveling companion, Sophie, stuck up a flirtation with one of The Lakshmi Boys. She was on the balcony, drying her hair. He was on the terrace near the restaurant. They called to each other across a chasm. The subject of age came up. Hers went down, his went up—an agreement seemed to have been reached. That night, we were eating at the restaurant and he joined us at our table. This, it seems, was part of the agreement. Sadly, up close, he was not what he had seemed across the chasm.

"Why didn't you tell me?" she hissed. "I didn't have my glasses on when I started this!" I laughed and kept a silence as inscrutable as the night, or so I imagined. I looked at the fabulous stars and kept quiet, listening to the sound of those waves rolling into the dark shore while Sophie dealt with the would-be Romeo who had failed so miserably to live up to expectations, even in such an extraordinary place and time.

Obnoxious as they can be, there is a certain pathos about The Lakshmi Boys. It doesn't take much to turn them from swaggering Romeo to obsequious boy. I can't claim to have felt any real remorse for having involved this particular Lakshmi Boy in the saga of the plastic chair, but I did feel a little guilt, just a tiny sliver of it and then only for a moment. He was a particularly bad specimen who, despite the evening's events (or non-events), took to hanging around our terrace and sulking for lack of attention. After a few days, I'd had enough and frightened him off by promising a visit from a large and fearsome husband. He disappeared quickly enough, but he was to reappear again, because of the chair.

It had become my habit to take a chair up to the rooftop terrace in the mornings in order to watch the glorious sunrise in some comfort. The chair came down with me to our room and went up to the terrace again in the evenings when the sun was setting. This coming and going meant negotiating a set of narrow concrete steps, and it wasn't so bad when you were going up, holding the chair in front of you. In fact, there was something reassuring about having the chair as a kind of shield. But coming down was another story. I am generally not good with heights, and something about the angle of descent, coupled with the fact that the chair was occupying my hands so that I could not reach out and grab a rail or steady myself against the wall, made me very nervous, until I solved the problem. My solution was a stroke of genius. It was simple and effective. Before descending from the rooftop, I threw the chair over the edge to the lower terrace. The first few times it hit the terrace on its side with a nice bounce. No harm done. On the last occasion, the night before we left Mahabalipuram, it crashed with an unusual thwack. I inspected the poor chair, only to find a crack along the left back leg. Long periods of exposure to the elements had made the plastic hard and brittle. I sat down in the chair, rocked back and forth, tempting fate, but fate would not be tempted, so I assumed all was well with the chair. In its present state, it was no better and no worse than most of the chairs scattered around Lakshmi Lodge, and I thought no more about it.

In the morning, there was a great fuss outside our door. We staggered out into the light to see The Boy dramatically pointing to the damaged chair and threatening us with the police if we did not immediately pay 500 rupees. He was very angry. My response was ineffectual because, I am ashamed to say, I found the scene quite enticing. I breathed in the sea air and watched the drama unfold, feeling like someone who has secured a free front-row seat to the opera. To my delight, my companion, disillusioned as she had been with the romantic prospects offered by The Lakshmi and The Boy, in particular, was ready for a confrontation.

"I will not deal with you," she said, scathingly, and demanded to see the owner of the establishment. She had scored a point. The price for the chair went down a little, but the word "police" flew about the Lakshmi like an enraged mynah bird.

An audience was gathering. I became increasingly delighted by the scene before me and watched my friend with pride as she slammed her fist theatrically on the little outdoor table and declared that she was about to lose her temper, so that there could be no mistaking her mood. That she could do this without laughing was beyond me. Bravissima! I needed to sit down, so I grabbed the nearest chair and sat on it. Of course, it was the chair in question. The Boy took this as a direct challenge. He had never quite believed in my "husband," but had erred on the side of caution. I am sure he held a grudge, feeling that he would have had a real chance with Sophie but for my presence. With a dark glance in my direction, he stormed off down the stairs to fetch "the owner." Soon, he returned, accompanied by someone who was clearly not the owner but was certainly higher in the pecking order of the Lakshmi. He was a pleasant enough man in a clean dhoti with the religious mark on his forehead. We recognized him as the man who had met us when we jumped off the bus from Chennai. It was he who had led us along the back paths of Mahabalipuram to the Lakshmi, making sure we were not tempted by any other guesthouse on the way. With his beard and his beads, he had the look of a sadhu rather than of a Lakshmi Boy.

"I want to settle this pleasantly," said my friend.

"I want to be friendly," said he.

So far, so good. I rocked a little in the chair. And then the negotiations began.

"I cannot see," he said gently, casting a sad look in my direction as if he knew the real nature of the wrongdoing and where the blame lay, "how the wind could have blown this chair down from the roof of your room."

Sophie had explained that the chair had been the victim of

natural forces rather than of any willful act of carelessness. His dark eyes looked skyward, and I felt he had made a point and that perhaps his silent pact with God would lead to my undoing. But, unimpeded by my spineless weakness, Sophie straightened in her own chair and managed to look particularly haughty. Above reproach. Queen Victoria would have been proud.

"It was a gale," she said firmly. I tried to show no surprise at this interesting turn of events. "We were afraid for our lives," she said dramatically. I admired her excess and tried to look suitably timid, like a woman who has just survived a hurricane.

In the meantime, The Boy had switched from rage to whining. I watched him with something bordering on compassion. Somewhere in the back of my mind, the realization dawned that the reparation for the damage would not come out of the owner's pocket, no matter how old the chair was. It would be extracted from The Boy's meager salary, in one chunk or bit by bit, like rotten teeth from an old mouth. But I also knew that it was very unlikely that the damage would be reported to the owner or ever found out. It was a simple matter of exchanging the damaged chair with the one propped in the darkest corner of the room, where it would remain unused and unnoticed unless the Lakshmi reverted to being a brothel again. And then, who knows what might happen to the chairs, or to The Boy, for that matter! In any event, time was moving on, we had a bus to catch, and we settled the matter amicably and rather generously, considering the hardship we had suffered during the night's tempest. Later, in the markets of Pondicherry, we came across the plastic chair, a new version, of course, and it cost around 200 rupees, and that before bargaining! We had handed over a cool 300 to the Lakshmi Boys. When all was said and done, the negotiator and The Boy had done very well out of my vertigo. Or perhaps the negotiator did have something going with his God, after all.

# LOST AND FOUND IN RUSSIA
Judy S. Richardson

*Taking a new step, uttering a new word, is what people fear most.* —Dostoyevsky

I was fifteen in 1960 when Khrushchev banged his shoe on a table at the United Nations. The USSR was our enemy in 1960. We practiced duck and cover drills in high school hallways, using the opportunity to socialize—what did we care about bombs? No way I ever wanted to visit Russia.

In the 1990s, Gorbachev's policies of perestroika and glasnost introduced restructuring and openness to travel between the USA and Russia. We were all friends now, for one glorious decade.

I befriended a professor from a Russian university on exchange at my university. When Luda invited me to lecture in her country for a month, I accepted. In October of 1999, I boarded a plane to Moscow, waving goodbye to my husband and three sons. On the airplane, I tried tracking my flight and the path to Nizhny Novgorod, my final destination, but the map tracker showed my city not northwest of Moscow, but southwest. I was lost and had not even landed.

"Ah, it is because of spies," the flight attendant shrugged. Air maps disguised closed cities, such as Nizhny Novgorod had been until recently. I was not lost, but suddenly a bit chilly.

The Sheremetyevo airport loomed huge and dingy. Jetlagged, I stumbled along in the line to passport control. We stopped, started, and jostled. A young woman in front of me turned and whispered, "Where are you from?"

I told her Richmond, Virginia. "And you?"

"I'm from Lansing, Michigan. Don't tell anyone." Before I could ask why that should be a secret, she went on. "My husband and I have $10,000 in cash on us. Because we're going to adopt a baby."

"Oh! That's a lot. Be careful." I did not want to be part of this secret.

"We're allowed that much, but I'm so nervous about Customs."

Her husband turned around. "Shh, Carol. Be quiet."

I followed them until the line divided at four booths. When I reached baggage claim, they had vanished—I hoped on their way to the orphanage and not to jail. I struggled with my two suitcases and searched for Luda, who was waiting behind the ropes for me.

She whisked me into the backseat of a taxi. "Do you have some U.S. dollars?"

"Yes." I tugged at my fanny pack.

"It is not allowed, but it the best way to pay. Put five dollars on the front seat, but out of view of passersby."

The driver placed his hand over the bills and swept them into his pocket. We began our whirlwind five-hour tour of Moscow. I pinched myself to stay awake after so many hours in the air. In our compartment on the train that evening, I was startled to find four beds, two occupied by men. I didn't undress. I fell asleep quickly to the noises of the lurching train.

Locked Up

I stayed near Gorky Square, a neighborhood of shops over which Gorky's statue presided. During the Communist era, the city had been renamed in honor of the Soviet writer; the statue and square still honored him. My apartment building was down the street, off the third alley, and through a battered steel door set into a mustard-yellow cement building. I climbed five sets of 20 steps each—no lift. An all-purpose living-dining-sleeping room led to a balcony that sagged so badly I would not step onto it. The view of tin roofs and dusty streets was not worth a fall.

During my first week, Luda protected me to the point of irritation. She introduced herself to my three neighbors and instructed them to "look after me." I never saw them again. Luda showed up at my door daily by nine. She walked me back each afternoon and insisted that I practice locking and unlocking my metal door until she was satisfied with my skills. I needed to jiggle the large key just so, turn counter and then clockwise to a certain degree before I heard the click. Some evenings, Luda waited for as much as twenty minutes before I was successful. And then, I did this set of motions backward in the mornings, from inside the door. For that first week, I didn't want to go out after she left, fearful I would not get in again and spend the night on the landing. I listened until I heard the last of her steps echoing away and the outer door of the building clanging shut before I settled in for the evening.

Lost in Darkness

Because the apartment was two miles from the university building, we walked or took the trolley. During the commute, Luda would chide, "Don't smile. Don't walk so fast. People will know you're American."

"Is that bad?" I asked.

"We don't draw attention to ourselves."

One evening, deep darkness met us as we entered my building. The light sockets held no bulbs.

"People take them," Luda explained. "Like the toilet paper."

I was prepared, though. I fished a small torch from my purse to guide us up the stairs.

Another evening, Luda took me to meet her dear friend, a retired professor who lived far out of the city. We rode a train and a bus, then walked many blocks to arrive at her apartment.

The woman let us in after Luda spoke a code word and fastened three locks. Her home was dark, only one lamp on in her living room. She sat across from me, the chairs so close our knees touched, and held my hands. Her voice was low; I strained to hear her. She talked of persecution, of her American friend who had lived in the USSR and helped the government for years but ended in Siberia.

All was not well in this new Russia. Yeltsin's market economy had bankrupted citizens who, like Luda, now stuffed cash in mattresses. Putin hovered in the wings. "He is our only choice," my colleagues opined.

Finding My Way

Luda decided, after 10 days, that I was capable of finding my own way. Released, I walked from the university back to Gorky Square alone. I hurried past a building set back from the road—KGB? Those windows no longer had eyes, I had been assured, but I felt watched as I shivered by. To calm my nerves, I stopped and gazed at the convergence of the Olka and the Volga. I window-shopped on Prokavska Street. Then I turned onto my side street and down a familiar-looking alley. But this was not my alley. I backtracked three times before I found my way.

I had mastered steel doors; I could light the pilot hidden in a cabinet over the stove and boil enough water daily for drinking and cooking. I knew how to navigate the market of vendors selling slabs of raw, uncovered meat or freshly wilting vegetables. I could find my way home.

Lost Riding with Strangers

In my third week, I went on a wild and crazy ride.

"You are going to visit the business college," Luda informed me, opening the door to a black car in front of the university.

By now I expected sudden changes in my schedule, so I slid in and over to make room for Luda, who closed the door and waved me off. Dismayed, I watched her disappear from view as the driver pulled away. Yes, I had been annoyed by her protectiveness, but suddenly she had deserted me. I was on my own; I didn't know where I was going and this adventure might not go well.

I said "hello"/ "Zdravstvuj" to the driver, his passenger in front, and the stout man beside me. No response. The car was steamy—Russians keep everything inside too hot. I was sweaty and nervous. Why hadn't Luda come with me? Who were these guys? Could they be Russian agents? Had I committed some suspicious act or made some unfortunate remark? All things considered, I did not want to be in this car. The driver slowed down so I edged nearer to the door. But when he stopped—in the middle of the road—the door opened from outside and a fourth man climbed in. No choice now but to squeeze myself into the middle. We swayed as the car careened in and out of traffic, tires screeching, cars swerving. Someone smelled rank, probably me. For twenty minutes, I gripped my briefcase and thought about my family and the good life I had had.

My head banged against the front seat when the driver screeched to an abrupt stop. The man who had joined us jumped out, held his hand to me and said, "Here, lady." I tested my feet to see if I could stand without collapsing. He escorted me into the college.

Eleanor Roosevelt advised, "Do one thing every day that scares you." I did, but not on purpose.

Lost in St. Petersburg, Russia

Lectures ended, I joined a group of tourists at the Soviet-style Hotel Pribaltiyskaya on the Baltic Sea in St. Petersburg. My window, grimy with dirt, let in very little light and not much of a view. I tried spit, and then soap, but the patch I made in the opaqueness didn't help much.

Guards checked my passport and room key before I could catch an elevator. I wrote notes on the back of the hotel card so I could find my way to my floor and onto the right hall. No room service or coffee supplies were available so I boiled water for instant coffee using my immersion heater. The lights in my room blew; in fact, the entire hall went dark. Then the knock came on my door. The repair was quick; my embarrassment was longer lasting. The hall housekeeper motioned me to her tiny closet, showed me a pot of hot water, and gestured that I come to her next time.

We visited the usual grand places: the bridges, the Church of the Spilt Blood, Peterhof Museum Reserve, St. Isaac's Cathedral, Catherine's Palace, and the Winter Palace. I had my picture taken with The Bronze Horseman and at the McDonald's. In The Hermitage, we walked through rooms and rooms of art.

On the last the morning of the tour, the rest of my group departed, but the guide kindly drove me into the city and dropped me at Dostoyevsky's apartment- museum.

"You will be fine here. Everyone speaks English. Take the green line back to the hotel."

Of course, no one at the museum spoke English. I wandered through the home where Dostoyevsky had penned his novels. When I hit the street two hours later, I was lost. I asked a passerby for Nevsky Prospekt. He did not speak English but beckoned for me to follow. We walked past the Grand Hotel. I saw the blue "M." At the ticket kiosk, I showed my hotel brochure to the clerk, who did not speak English. He nodded, sold me a ticket, and pointed toward a platform. On the train, I asked the man beside me for help. He peered at my map and said, "Okay." Was that reassurance? I decided it must be. I sat tight as we sped through the dark tunnel. When we came into light on the island of Vasileyvsky Ostrov, he tapped me.

"Da. Do svidanija!" / "Yes. Goodbye!"

"Spasibo!" I thanked him and exited at Vasileostovskaya (no, I can't pronounce it). The place did not look familiar, but I trudged along Stredny Prospekt until I saw Nalichnaya Boulevard, which was on my tiny hotel map. I was near! Turning left on Nakhimova, I caught a glimpse of the Baltic Sea and rushed towards the hotel. The Primorskaya station would have been much closer. But I had found my way.

Found in Helsinki, Finland

The next day, the train streamlined me to Helsinki. When the Russian patrol debarked and a Finnish Border Guard asked for my passport, I smiled. My body relaxed from a tension I had been carrying for four weeks. In Helsinki, the train emptied quickly. I lugged my suitcase into a rainy night. Like a bug, I followed the neon light to the Sokus Hotel. The clerk welcomed me in English. On my one full day in Helsinki, I visited the Sibelius monument, awed by those 600 steel pipes. I listened to Finlandia, which I knew as By Still, My Soul. In fact, this melody's title has changed often, at first to avoid Russian censorship in the early 1900s. I stood in front of Eila Hiltunen's Passio Musicae, smiling into a camera. I was almost home.

# HITCHHIKER
Joe Albanese

I sit in a parked car,
a rolling stone in a movement ceased
I laughed, I coughed, I screamed
at what we really need in the lives we lease

Just shoes and the next road
I think I smoked what the homeless dream
A have in loss, it seems
a run away to some, to others a sip of tea

I'm tired for just a seed
A burning home is just a redesign
There's a million miles of me —
an out of time, a feelin' fine

I couldn't count the scars
To travel the world is to traverse your fears
I hitchhike through those seas:
a stormy when, a never be

My thumb out on the street
but no one answers that sotto plea
More coffee and some cream
So much to do, more than we see.

# THE VOMIT COMET TO KOH TAO
Fahy Brennen

I awoke to a pounding on my door that echoed the pounding in my head. I stumbled out of bed and peeled open the door, doing my best to shield myself with it from the bright Thai sun. I was greeted by the hostel manager as he wedged his face into the gap between the door and began to screech at me, informing me that I had slept past checkout time and that I needed to leave immediately. I told him that I was sorry and that I would be right down, and began to pack my bag. It was the morning after the Full Moon Party on Koh Phan Ngan, and I was in rough shape.

I gathered my bag and sat down in the hostel's small restaurant to order a much-needed coffee. I looked at some of the patrons around me and felt a perverse pleasure in seeing that my fellow travelers were in just as poor condition as I was. A gang of Australian men, who probably hadn't been to bed yet, sent a round of breakfast beers over to a group of queasy-looking British women still covered in neon paint from the night before. The beers were politely sent back and I wondered if the Aussies would have had more luck if they sent had over a round of Tylenol.

I settled my bill with the hostel and hailed a cab. It dropped me off at the docks, and I bought a ticket for the ferry ride to Koh Tao, the next destination on my trip through South East Asia. The population on the island of Koh Phan Ngan can quadruple for the monthly beach party. I had anticipated an exodus of people trying to get off the island, so I arrived at the ferry terminal early. I took a seat on a bench and waited as crowds of hung-over travelers staggered out of cabs and bought ferry tickets to the mainland and the surrounding islands.

The departure time for my ferry was fast approaching, but as I scanned the waters around the docks, I couldn't see any vessels on the horizon. I couldn't see any ships at all besides a thin boat that was struggling to moor itself to the dock as waves batted it around like a leaf. It wasn't until people started loading their bags into it that I realized it was my ride to Koh Tao. I was more than a little surprised; the ferry that took me to Koh Phan Ngan from the mainland was a monster. It wasn't exactly the Titanic, but it had twin smokestacks and plowed through the ocean like a battering ram. The boat that pulled up to take me to Koh Tao looked more like a canoe with a jet engine strapped to it.

The sailors managed to get their ropes looped on the cleats and threw old rubber tires along the side of the boat to protect it as the ocean tried to dash it against the dock. With their vessel as securely tied as possible, they raised a rickety board and started loading up with hung-over and nervous riders.

On unsteady legs, I walked down the gangplank and wiggled into one of the seats with my fellow passengers. Most of them, including myself, still smelling sour from the night before. We were given a brief safety demonstration in Thai that no one understood and, before we knew it, the boat was roaring toward the open ocean. It fought bravely against the waves, but once it left the shelter of the island's reef, it began to struggle against the swells. The climb up each wave and the inevitable slide down the other side turned the ocean into a seemingly infinite roller coaster, and passengers that were only a little queasy before turned an alarming shade of green. I was fine, for a while, but soon the waves got to me as well, and within half an hour, most of the passengers were volcanoes of misery and nausea. There were limited numbers of barf bags to go around, and any maritime code of conduct regarding women and children first was hurled over the side like so many breakfasts as a free-for-all began for the remaining bags. Those without tried to improvise with plastic bags and small paper cups, and when those ran out, I began to notice streamlets of puke running down the deck and between my sandaled feet. The smell was horrible, and I came close to throwing up myself. I closed my eyes and rested my forehead against the warm plastic of the seat in front of me, and tried to shut out the terrible scene around me, but I could still hear the retches and mewling of the weak, lacking the courtesy to suffer in silence like the rest of us.

I remained in that position for most of the trip. I began to feel a little better and opened my eyes, hoping to see our destination on the horizon. I didn't see Koh Tao, but what I did see almost made me throw up right then and there. Men and women, who hadn't slept in days, clutched plastic bags filled with the contents of their stomachs like dripping purses. People took turns doing the Technicolor yawn outside the few portholes in the cabin, and the whole time vomit sloshed back and forth with the rise and fall of the waves. The level of spew splashing about on the cabin deck had gotten to such a level that I feared we would soon have to grab buckets and start bailing before we were sunk.

I started looking around for potential bail buckets, but every basin, bowl, cup, urn, tin, and container capable of holding liquid was already filled with people's regurgitated groceries. Luckily, it never came to that because one of the passengers, undoubtedly staring out to sea and considering jumping in to end the whole emesis filled nightmare, spotted a dot on the horizon.

"I see it! I think I see Koh Tao!" they cried.

And everyone let out a collective groan of relief. I looked out the window and saw the dot and watched it grow until it jutted out of the middle of the ocean like a jade jewel. Warm golden beaches ringed it and colorful fishing boats circled it like satellites. It was beautiful. I would have been filled with awe if I weren't already completely topped up with nausea.

Our boat steered into the calm, protected waters of the island's bay and nestled against the dock with the gentlest of bumps. The crew raised the beam to the dock and their half-dead cargo of passengers began to disembark. I crawled across the gangplank, brushed a spot clear of cigarette butts, and flopped onto the dock. I reveled in the solid ground and promised myself I would never drink again.

Well, maybe not until the next full moon.

# FARMER JOE
Ruyi Wen

Farmer Joe shook his head in disappointment when he saw the headline of the morning paper lying on the breakfast table: *Turkish Terrorist Captured on Capitol Hill!*

"What is the world coming to?" he sighed. "You'd think those damned foreigners would learn that what's good for the United States of America is good for everyone! Except maybe those people in third-world countries, and they don't count. They're not even American citizens!"

Joe Miller was an Indianan soybean farmer who believed in rugged individualism, the Protestant work ethic, and the government's responsibility to aid ailing agriculturalists. This last belief was the most firmly rooted in his philosophy, as Farmer Joe was the largest non-grower of soybeans in the state. Through a shrewd marriage to a senator's daughter, he had managed to secure farm subsidies on all the land that he left fallow. This, Farmer Joe was convinced, was for the good of the country, since there was no demand for soybeans anyway. But Farmer Joe wasn't greedy. Instead of hoarding the money, he generously gave it back to the government in exchange for more land with which not to grow soybeans. The government was so pleased with Farmer Joe's tireless efforts for the good of the country that it gave him a monopoly on the domestic soybean market.

Farmer Joe skimmed the article about the terrorist and would have quickly moved onto the funnies page if the word soybeans in the article had not caught his attention. The newspaper reported that the terrorist, a woman—*highly unusual*—had not only given American military secrets to ISIS but was known to eat organic soybeans, a practice so clearly un-American that the government was surprised it had not caught her earlier. Farmer Joe perked up at this news.

"This is the second article I've read this month about terrorism," he mused, "And in that time, I've only seen one article about Oklahoma. My God, that must mean there are twice as many terrorists in the country as Oklahomans! And if this lady eats organic soybeans, then imagine all the demand there is for organic soybeans by the terrorists in the country!" Visions of staggering wealth danced in Joe's head like sugarplum fairies. "I've got to get in on this organic soybean market! There's some real money to be made there!"

As it turned out, Farmer Joe's monopoly on the domestic soybean market also covered the market for organic soybeans. Farmer Joe immediately stopped not growing regular soybeans and put all his land into disuse, not growing organic soybeans. The conversion was quite simple, as none of the soybean plants that Joe didn't have had ever been treated with pesticides. The government was pleased to learn of this development, for there was even less demand for organic soybeans than for regular soybeans, and the price of organic soybeans was three times the price of regular soybeans, which meant triple the tax the government could collect from all the organic soybeans Farmer Joe didn't sell.

"Whaddya mean, my order will be shipped immediately?" Frankie screamed into the phone. "I've never gotten a shipment of soybeans from you before! What's wrong now? I have customers who are counting on me as the most reliable non-server of soybean foods in the city!"

"Sorry, but the market's hot for organic foods," the wholesaler explained. "If you want organic soybeans, I wouldn't have any to ship to you. But regular soybeans are a dime a bushel now."

"Organic soybeans!" Frankie snapped. "Who wants organic

soybeans?"

"No one," the wholesaler replied. "That's why there's such a great supply of organic soybeans not getting shipped to us by a farmer in Indiana who's got a monopoly on the market. And these organic soybeans are going at three times the price."

"But wh—did you say *three* times the price?"

"Yes, sir. It takes much more time and money to grow organic soybeans, you know. Alternatives to not spraying chemicals and not using artificial fertilizers are very expensive. That's why they're going for three times the price."

Frankie may have only been the owner of a small diner, but he was no idiot when it came to macroeconomics. "Three times the price? Cancel my order on the regular soybeans. I want a dozen cases of organic soybeans here by tomorrow!"

"You won't get them, sir."

"Good!" Frankie said triumphantly, slamming down the receiver.

Frankie's diner was a favorite among Washington bureaucrats who hated foreign, unpatriotic foods such as soybeans, couscous, and French fries. In twenty years of operation, Frankie's diner had never been known to serve a single soy smoothie with extra wheatgrass, and it was for this reason that Allen Kater, who ordered a soy smoothie with extra wheatgrass for lunch every day, liked Frankie's diner so much.

Kater was a high-level intelligence agent whose primary responsibility was delegating work that he couldn't do to subordinates. Since he was not intelligent enough to do any of the work assigned to him, he performed his job superbly. Agent Kater was also constantly on a diet. His doctor had recommended soy smoothies once a day to reduce his cholesterol level, but his doctor was from Turkey. Or Turkmenistan. Kater knew it was somewhere in the Middle East, or at least Middle East-adjacent. And Kater didn't trust the Middle East because it was full of Arabs, and wasn't the military busy with airstrikes on Arabian-speaking Syrians right now? Kater slammed his fist on his desk. He was a patriotic, hardworking, honest-to-goodness American, and he'd be damned if he was going to take advice from an enemy of the state.

Agent Kater looked at his watch. It was nearly noon. He had been at work for almost two hours, signing papers stamped *Top Secret* and sending them down a chute labeled *High Security*, which led to an incinerator in a basement room with three padlocks on the door. Agent Kater felt his stomach grumble. It had been three hours since his doctor-recommended breakfast of eggs Benedict, bacon, and buttermilk pancakes. Actually, the breakfast his doctor had recommended was Cheerios and orange juice, but that just further proved that his doctor was an enemy of the state. Weren't Cheerios British? Or at least something the British liked to say? And hadn't America gone to war with Britain at least twice, and against Britain at least twice more? Kater slammed his fist on his desk. He was a patriotic, hardworking, honest-to-goodness American, and he'd be damned if he was going to take advice from a Middle Eastern insurgent who supported an enemy of the United States.

Agent Kater's stomach grumbled again. He had been so unselfishly devoted to his work that he had nearly forgotten about lunch while contemplating the issue of terrorism. He briskly walked to Frankie's Diner down the street and took his usual seat at the bar.

"Soy smoothie," he said to Frankie. "Extra wheatgrass."

Every day for the past three years, Kater had ordered a soy smoothie with extra wheatgrass at Frankie's for lunch, and every day for the past three years, Frankie had replied that he was out of soy smoothies. Kater would then sigh, and, proud that he was following such a healthy diet, order a consolation freedom burger with freedom chili fries. Kater, always eager to do something for the good of the country, considered it his patriotic duty to eat freedom burgers and freedom chili fries whenever soy smoothies were in short supply, since it further promoted the non-production of soybeans, which he considered a subversive crop, liable to be used by communists in biochemical weapons or whatever.

Today, however, Frankie plunked down a tall glass of greenish-white liquid on the counter in front of Kater.

Kater blinked in surprise and stared at the glass. "What's this?" he asked.

"Soy smoothie, extra wheatgrass."

"What? But I thought you didn't sell soy smoothies because you couldn't get any soybeans!"

"Well, there's no market for regular soybeans anymore," explained Frankie. "The whole country's going for organic food. No one's not growing regular soybeans anymore. All the farmers are tripping over themselves to not produce organic soybeans now. Drives up the price, you know. Too bad there's a monopoly on the market, though."

"But can't you still not serve regular soybeans?"

"Sorry, Al, but I've gotten out of that business. Now I'm only not serving organic soybeans. If you want an organic soy smoothie, it'd be three times the price of a regular soy smoothie, only I won't have any."

"Organic soybeans?" Kater gasped. "But who wants organic soybeans?"

Frankie shrugged. "Lots of people, I guess. It's such a hot crop, no one can get their hands on any."

"Organic soybeans," Kater repeated. "That sounds pretty suspicious to me. Don't you think organic foods are un-American?"

"Nah. Organic soybeans are being not grown all over Indiana. You can't get much more American than Indiana."

Kater was dismayed. Not only did he have to order organic soy smoothies from now on, he had to pay three times the money for them, and on a government salary, too! He sipped at his unappetizing soy smoothie, hungry and annoyed. And when Kater was annoyed, he took his wrath out on the nearest possible bystander, which, in this case, was a young woman, barely out of her teens, sitting a few seats down. She was sorrowfully looking at an empty glass in front of her on the counter.

"What's that woman doing?" Kater whispered to Frankie. "The one sitting over there, not drinking anything."

"Oh, that's Sisi," said Frankie. "Nice girl. German. Works for some hotshot diplomat up on Embassy Row, I think. Been coming in for my organic soy smoothies every morning for the last few months. I hate to disappoint her like this, suddenly not selling organic soy smoothies, but hey, if not planting organic soybeans is the American way, then not selling organic soybeans is my patriotic duty."

Kater ruminated upon this. If not selling organic soybeans was patriotic, and this woman drank organic soy smoothies, then…she must be an enemy of the state! Kater narrowed his eyes suspiciously. Now that he thought about it, SISI was an anagram for ISIS. It was also ISIS backwards and upside down. You couldn't spell terrorist without I-S. And you couldn't spell Sisi without them either! That settled the matter. Sure, terrorists weren't usually blonde and blue-eyed women, but after a mandatory sensitivity training Kater had undergone at work for making some perfectly justifiable and anthropologically accurate comments about Mongoloids, he had learned that racial profiling was wrong. Anyone could be a terrorist if they worked hard and believed in their dreams.

Kater tapped the young woman on the shoulder. "Ma'am, please come with me."

The young woman blinked in surprise. "Who are you?" she asked in a slight German accent.

Kater whipped out his FBI badge. "If I told you, I would have to kill you. You may call me Agent Kater. Now come with me."

Sisi started to get up from her seat.

"Freeze right there!" Kater screamed. "No sudden movements!" He slapped a pair of handcuffs on the woman and glared at her. "I thought we could do this the easy way, but if you're not going to cooperate, then you leave me no choice."

He dragged the woman back to his office and looked her up on his computer. Elisabeth "Sisi" Fischer had been born in Hamburg, which made her a Hamburger. Very suspicious, Kater thought. She was undoubtedly related to the notorious criminal The Hamburglar. And Germans, as a whole, weren't to be trusted. Hadn't America gone to war either with them or against them several times? And wasn't Germany a hotbed of terrorism nowadays? It had taken in all those Turkish refugees, who were now driving trucks into crowded plazas and sexually assaulting the local women. How could anyone be sure that this Sisi Fischer wasn't one of those German refugee terrorists, mowing down innocent civilians and groping high school girls? Kater shuddered at Sisi's treachery. And he did not fail to note that her last name, Fischer, had an I-S in it as well. Proof again!

"Sir?" Sisi asked apprehensively.

"What?" Kater snapped irritably.

"Um... are you not going to ask me any questions?"

"What do you think I'm doing now?"

"But you have asked me nothing."

"Oh, I've found out plenty. You're a Turkish terrorist, aren't you?"

"What? No! I am not even from the Turkey. I am German. I am here, in this country, working as an au pair."

"An oper…what? Operations analyst? Opera singer?"

"Au pair," Sisi repeated. "It is like, how you call it, nanny—"

"Oh, God, an operative!" Kater screamed. "I knew it! Frankie said you worked for some foreign official! You're some kind of secret agent here to steal our government secrets and bomb the shit out of our country! That's it. You're under arrest!"

"What? Why am I arrested?"

"Espionage! You've been selling secrets to ISIS, haven't you? I bet you've been tampering with my correspondence, too. That's why I never see any of my papers after I sign them! You ought to be hanged, shot, and electrocuted for your treachery!"

"Mr. Kater! I have not—"

"How did you know my name?"

"What? You said your name is Agent Kater."

"Don't lie to me! I would have given you an undercover alias! No matter. The fact you spied on me to find out my real identity is just more proof of your subversive activities."

"What are you talking about? What does subversive activities mean?"

"Hey, who's asking the questions here, you or me?"

"You… well, I—"

"Just keep your mouth shut while I call headquarters and have them throw the book at you. Any requests for a particular book? Kafka, perhaps? Or a lovely volume by Günter Grass?"

"Wait! But I have done nothing! Do I not get a lawyer?"

"Dammit! I said I'm asking the questions around here! Besides, you have no rights if you've been convicted of treason."

"But I have not been convicted of treason!"

"Are you contradicting me?"

"No—well, yes. I am!"

"Aha! So you admit it! You're guilty! Guilty as hell! Only an insurgent bent on destroying the greatest country in the world would contradict its government agents, who are the voice of its people and the soul of its bureaucracy!" Kater yanked up the phone receiver. "Headquarters! This is Agent Kater. I've captured a terrorist!"

Headquarters, which had been making so little headway on its various domestic and foreign quagmires, was ecstatic to hear of this unexpected victory in the war on terror. The next day, newspapers across the country ran headline stories about

Sisi Fischer, denouncing her as a terrorist spy who not only sold military secrets to ISIS but also engaged in unpatriotic activities such as eating organic soybeans and being a Turkish refugee. Sisi Fischer was promptly shipped off to a detainment camp in Cuba and Agent Kater was promoted to a position in which he no longer even had to delegate work.

Farmer Joe shook his head in disappointment when he saw the headline of the morning paper lying on the breakfast table: *Turkish Terrorist Captured on Capitol Hill!*

"What is the world coming to?" he sighed. "You'd think those damned foreigners would learn that what's good for the United States of America is good for everyone!"

# A CONVERSATION WITH DIETRICH KALTEIS

*Lowestoft Chronicle* (November 2017)

Eight years ago, Dietrich Kalteis was a new fiction writer, contributing short stories to a variety of familiar literary magazines, including the *Lowestoft Chronicle*. Now, he is fast becoming one of Canada's top modern crime writers. His debut novel, *Ride the Lightning*, won an Independent Publishers Award and was hailed as one of the best Vancouver crime novels, and he has since gone on to pen four more gritty, noteworthy crime novels that have had people comparing him to the likes of Elmore Leonard. *Publishers Weekly* have called his books fast-moving, high-octane page-turners full of well-drawn characters and authentic-sounding dialogue, and the *National Post* has praised him for his plot structure and breezy style. As *The Globe and Mail* put it, when discussing his gloriously hard and fast style: "If you like hard sex, tough talk, motorcycles, guns and boys with toys, this is your meat."

Dietrich Kalteis (Photography: Andrea Kalteis)

In an exclusive interview with *Lowestoft Chronicle*, Kalteis talks about his novels, his literary influences, and some of his many future projects.

**Lowestoft Chronicle (LC):** Your latest crime novel, *Zero Avenue*, is getting a lot of much-deserved attention, with positive reviews from readers and the likes of *Publishers Weekly* and *Kirkus Reviews*. Did you get a sense while writing it that it would prove popular?

**Dietrich Kalteis (DK):** I had no idea how the book would be received while I was writing it. I don't think a story would work if I tried to plot it out based on what I thought would be a hit. I write what appeals to me, the kind of story that I'd like to read myself. My stories usually stem from something I've heard, read, experienced or dreamed up. Then I think, what if this happens, and I give it a twist. Starting with a single scene, I drop in the type of characters I'd like to have handle it, and I see where it goes, letting the story unfold as the scenes and characters develop.

**LC:** Some years ago, you mentioned reading an article in the *National Post* about the billion-dollar cannabis industry in British Columbia. And, apparently, you knew some guys who tried to rob a pot field and had rock salt shot at them. Does *Zero Avenue* stem from those two stories?

**DK:** I chose the punk scene of the late seventies for the setting because it was so raw and angry, and Vancouver was such a polite, sleepy backwater town back then, so there was this natural tension. I always loved that story of the two guys getting rock salt shot at them, and I wanted to include it. There was no satellite imagery or Google Earth back then, and a pot field could stay hidden inside a cornfield.

That article about the billion-dollar cannabis industry sparked my first novel *Ride the Lightning*. It fascinated me how many grow-ops were estimated to be operating in secret, making pot one of the provinces leading cash crops, and all tax-free. I just had to spin a story around it.

**LC**: The early punk rock scene in British Columbia plays heavily into the narrative. What sort of research did you do into the punk era and drug trafficking in general?

**DK**: I was living in Toronto during those days, and I loved the punk scene. I talked to people who lived in Vancouver during those times. And there were some excellent books by John Armstrong (Buck Cherry of the Modernettes) and Joe Keithley (Joey Shithead of D.O.A), among others that made excellent reference. There was also a great documentary called *Bloodied but Unbowed* by Susanne Tabata, which helped with some of the details. And there was no shortage of archived news about smugglers and border jumpers on the drug trafficking front.

**LC**: Frankie del Rey, your kick-ass, punk rock protagonist, is a particularly striking character, not least because she's a tough, fist-swinging female caught up in a brutal, masculine world. How challenging was it writing from the female perspective while placing her in violent and vulnerable situations? And was it always your intention to have her be the main lead, rather than the club owner Johnny Falco?

**DK**: I wasn't sure at first if I could write a female lead character, but as Frankie's character took shape, I felt it was working, and she just started taking center stage. I like that both her and Johnny Falco have their own agendas, are unwitting and have to step up and face what comes at them.

**LC**: In 2014, you said: "When I'm writing, I always picture my stories like movie scenes and my characters like actors." It's often noted that there's a cinematic quality to your books. In fact, your screenplay, *Between Jobs*, was a finalist in the 2003 Los Angeles Screenplay Festival. Did you ever consider pursuing a career in screenwriting?

**DK**: I did pen a few screenplays some years ago, but writing novels allows more expression in the narrative, and time to build on details, characters, plot points, back stories and resolution. While I do visualize chapters like scenes in a film, and I like to let the characters tell much of the story through dialog, which works in either form, writing novels and screenplays are quite different. Although I've never seen myself writing screenplays as a career, it would be awesome to have one of my novels adapted and watch it come to life on the screen.

**LC**: In terms of the stories you read and write, you favor crime fiction over other literary genres. Was this always the case? Have you experimented with other genres and styles?

**DK**: When I started writing short stories I tried different genres to find where I fit. Once I found my voice, crime fiction just seemed to be where I belonged. Some of my stories border on historical fiction, but there's still a crime element. And while I read a lot of crime fiction, I also read outside the genre. It's about reading a great voice, and I'll read and reread just about anything by the likes of Hunter S. Thompson, Charles Bukowski, Patti Smith, Jack Kerouac, John Steinbeck, and J.D. Salinger.

**LC**: You've singled out authors like Elmore Leonard, George V. Higgins, James Crumley, Robert B. Parker, and Charles Willeford as writing novels you love. Are these the writers that have influenced you the most?

**DK**: They all had strong voices and wrote the kind of stories that I like. All were master storytellers who were great at writing dialog and adding levity to the tension. I could add a few more names to the list, like Don Winslow, Carl Hiaasen and James Ellroy, but writers of this caliber sure influence and inspire me to write at my personal best.

**LC:** You've had roughly fifty short stories published in literary magazines around the world. Did you make a conscious effort to switch to novel writing, or was this change because you felt *Ride the Lightning* merited more character and subplot development and would work better if expanded into novel form?

**DK:** At first, I experimented with different genres and approaches when I was writing primarily short stories, feeling I wasn't ready to tackle anything novel-length. One of the short stories I wrote was about an insurance investigator who gets into a relationship with a married woman who he's been taking pictures of. She tries to cheat the insurance company, but as sparks fly between them, his allegiance takes a shift. I really liked that piece and wanted to do more with it. I took the characters along with some ideas, which came after reading that news story about the billion-dollar pot industry, and it became a jumping-off point for *Ride the Lightning*.

**LC:** What is your writing process? Does the story come first or the character? I've heard you say that you don't work from an outline. Is that always the case?

**DK:** As the characters develop during a first draft, evolving from scene to scene, I let their nature dictate the course they're going to take, and I tell it from the character's point of view. The story just takes shape from an initial scene. I never outline a story; I just see where it goes. Ideas and situations come along that work into the story as I'm writing, and I think these turn out better than anything I could come up with if I sat down and outlined the story beforehand. Once I've got a first draft, I create a timeline and make sure everything makes sense and flows in a proper sequence. I also keep character sheets that contain information about each of them and help me keep facts straight.

**LC**: Given that you have five published novels under your belt, the next due for publication in June, and the first draft of another novel written out in longhand, has writing a novel become a smooth process for you? Is the eight months it took to write *Zero Avenue* the standard length of time it takes you to write a novel?

**DK**: Over the years I've found what works best for me, which includes switching off the phone and playing music through headphones to cut out any white noise. And I try to keep away from social media while I'm working. Also, my energy for writing is best when I start early in the morning, usually around five, then I write until noon. There are no fast rules about it, but I try to have one novel finished every year. Sometimes that comes easy, and other times a story needs extra work and time.

**LC**: ECW Press, a major independent book publisher in Canada, has published all of your novels. How did you get involved with this publisher? Did you approach other publishers when trying to place that first manuscript?

**DK**: I sent *Ride the Lightning* to a couple of agents and directly to ECW. When Jack David got back to me a couple of weeks later and proposed a deal, I was thrilled. It was the right move for me, and it's been great working with the folks at ECW over the years.

**LC**: You have work forthcoming in *Vancouver Noir*, a new anthology in Akashic Books' Noir Series. Will this be a new story? Will it feature any familiar characters—Frankie, perhaps?

**DK**: It's a fresh story with new characters. The story's called *Bottom Dollar*, and it's about a second-story man who tries to rip off a gangster who keeps a lot of cash hidden in his house.

Bent on revenge from a previous encounter, our burglar breaks in late one night and runs into the gangster's disgruntled girlfriend pointing a pistol at him. It looks like he's screwed, until she says: "Take me with you."

**LC**: Your next novel, titled *Poughkeepsie Shuffle*, due for release in 2018, is a gangland tale of gun smuggling in Toronto in the mid-eighties. What made you set it in the 1980s and did the story necessitate a switch from west to eastern Canada?

**DK**: I grew up in Toronto back when there was Sam the Record Man on Yonge Street, the Brunswick House, Honest Ed's, and Eaton's at the Eaton's Center. A lot of the story takes place in an area called the Junction, and I wanted to capture the urban landscape the way I remembered it. After I read a news article about a gun-smuggling ring operating from New York state, smuggling guns up into Canada, the story just took shape from there.

**LC**: "I always listen to music while I write, and I play what goes with what I'm working on," you once said. Is *Poughkeepsie Shuffle* set to a hip-hop or glam metal beat? You're currently working on a historical novel set in Kansas in the Dirty Thirties. Are you listening to folk music or swing jazz?

**DK**: The music has to suit the vibe of what I'm writing. For *Zero Avenue*, I listened to a lot of West Coast punk, which went with the general intensity of the story. For *Poughkeepsie Shuffle* it was old-school rock, and for my dustbowl story, I've been leaning to folk, bluegrass and early blues, and yes, some swing jazz. There's no golden rule to it, I just put on what I feel like, but I've always got something playing while I'm writing.

# DREAM JOB
AN Block

February was just about the worst month. *Ever,* I told what's-her-name.

Seriously? The month our son got married. Really?

I can't remember, I said, putting the fork with the lukewarm Rice-A-Roni on it down, but, um, uh.

You're starting to trail off again. She wagged her finger. To not finish your sentences.

You know, I pointed at her, you remind me of, er. Then I rubbed my chin. I'm sorry, it's my job, mostly.

This exchange just exacerbated some already seething spousal tensions. By the time I reconstructed what the problem with February was, a losing parlay on Super Bowl Fifty, my special angel had gone apoplectic, reciting a litany of all too familiar complaints. Every time she'd pause for breath, I hoped the list might be complete, but it was like a song with false endings, because she kept remembering new transgressions, the capper of which involved my misplacing things I needed for work on a daily basis and then scribbling notes full of exclamation points blaming her, until the evening came when she'd prove conclusively that it was all my fault.

Well, I'm not going to debate you, point for point, I said. It's because I'm over-tired and stressed out at work.

You've been milking that excuse for years.

Being married to you, who needs excuses? I mean, what's dinner with Lucille without at least one screaming fit?

She rose from the table, and things took a turn for the worse until the small bookcase she kept mostly empty for just this purpose got overturned. We surveyed the disorder, giggled together, and agreed to sit and have a civilized dialogue. Like mature adults, calmly, she ordered.

All right, I began, I'll admit I haven't been myself lately. I've been this other guy I don't even recognize.

Other guy! You've been an absent-minded professor since the day we met, but you're much worse now. Especially since you read the autobiography of that whiney misogynist who thinks he's too good to collect his Nobel Prize in person. That's some hero for a grown man to emulate!

Don't even go there, I warned. Say what you will about me, drag my good name through the mud, I told her, but this is an outrage. I'm putting my foot down, I tell you. This will not stand!

So much for the what-do-you-call-it. Dialogue.

So, as spring approached, I initiated a campaign to render Lucille speechless with my charm, to dazzle her with gifts and poems handwritten on lavender-scented papyrus notepaper celebrating happier times in the Nill household. To no avail. She just kept yapping nonstop about my shortcomings. Meanwhile, lack of sleep kept making me woozier and more forgetful. Then, I embarked on a sustained eating binge. Four prodigious meals per day, with lavish in-between snacking. Combined with a constitutional aversion to any form of exercise more vigorous than using a corkscrew, this major league chow fest resulted in substantial accruals of weight. Which, of course, unleashed torrents of pent-up ridicule, not only from my dear one but also from the other aggressive sales types where I work at Hockmere, Nishkin and Chynik. Of course, letting it slip that I supported one of Donald Trump's moves (no, not all of them!) ballooned into another relationship issue of seismic proportions. Lucille started to lash out about things that hadn't been mentioned in years. In contrast to me, she's got the memory of a bull elephant, and suddenly everything became fair game.

I'm exhausted from you already, she said one night. You and your weirdo sense of humor.

Such as?

You're so inappropriate. Remember after I gave birth, how you said what a miracle, incredible, but I'll be leaving town for a while now, get back in touch when the kid's able to play catch?

And, in retaliation for this decades-old lapse in judgment, she withdrew whatever shreds of sympathy or support remained for my current work malaise.

*Wah!* she said, whenever I brought it up. *Wah-wah!*

Do you even comprehend what I'm saying? I asked her. This junior guy, he's with Hockmere six months max, gives his presentation, it's like I'm sitting there listening to myself!

People steal your ideas, even your exact lines; yes, I get it. So? You're in the business world. What else is new, Adrian? It's a form of flattery.

But, listen to me.

Flattery! she said. You think eating poorly will solve anything? Maybe the time's come to consider switching jobs and getting yourself together. Maybe sales isn't a good fit for Adrian Nill at his age. I know it's not good for us as a couple. Why don't you get out of HNC altogether and go find some relationship management gig like the one you used to do when we were first dating? When we were happy.

Every once in a great while I have to give Lucille credit— the woman comes up with some absolutely out-of-the-box brilliant ideas.

Quit my thing-a-ma-jig? I asked. You think I actually could?

Why not? Go find some division of a company somewhere, she said, run by some New Age space shot with an HR background. Preferably a millennial.

As I said, pure brilliance!

The essentials of my new position consist of being a yes man, a glad-hander. Fullmer & Gong is one of those outfits with regularly scheduled painting parties, pie contests, trivia quizzes, and low stakes bingo games. Sometimes, we sit in circles, close our eyes, and appreciate our collective energies. Every day here has its cutesy nickname: Happy Monday, Agenda Free Tuesday, Cookie and Cake Wednesday, Mental Health Thursday, Casual Friday. I'm the guy they call in to kiss up to high net worth customers, but only after all else fails, because, somehow, I'm the one best able to speak their language.

My role is to make sure that these clients feel comfortable with the way we handle their money. Confidence is huge in this game. Buy in. So, I'm the closer; on the rare occasions where they push back, I spring into action. A few of our investors are somewhat high maintenance, and pretty much all have their eccentricities. Some need to be called every Monday at a specific time; others are okay with attending a once-a-year meeting or playing golf monthly. The job, in plain English, is cake. Because I don't have to even do any heavy lifting, I can delegate most of it to my staff.

Being a parasite (or "sales weasel" as we were affectionately known at Hockmere), able to coast on my well-honed sycophantic skill set, was thrilling. In the beginning, I focused all attention on schmoozing Marshall, the founder, and on pumping his CEO ego up, because it was abundantly clear that the work of my department had little impact on the company's actual success or strategic direction. Perfect! When the big guy would rail against government regulations, I'd be the one to jump in at an appropriate pause and say, Damn right, it's enough to turn you into a libertarian! Afterward, I'd slink down the corridor to my office, draw the curtains, put the sign up saying *Do Not Disturb…Genius At Work*, and surf the Internet. I had it licked. Finally, my dream job. I was rejuvenated. No stress. Lucille and I began to really enjoy life again.

At night, though my head would hit the pillow, sleep would not come. Two, two thirty, wide awake. I'm not really fat, I'd tell myself, instead of counting sheep. I'm just bloated. It's a water retention thing. Glandular. I started arriving at work bleary-eyed, and the forgetfulness problem compounded. Despite all the daily ha-ha's, I learned that not everyone felt ecstatic at Fullmer. Then, I found out I was becoming a major topic of conversation. Why? My status as the guru and high priest of looking busy while not doing a damn thing did not go unnoticed. People would ask: how does he get away with it? They began to make pilgrimages from different branches and departments to observe, trying to ascertain my secret powers. Soon, every nut on the payroll started camping out at my door.

Some would come in and expound outlandish theories. One wild-haired marketing director, who carried around a piece of torn blanket wherever she went, told me, to be really healthy and, therefore, productive, you have to eat tons and tons of clarified homemade beef broth. My whole apartment reeks of it. Yes, sure it's disgusting, especially the jelly, but the nutritional therapist recommended that whatever your weight is in pounds, drink half of that in ounces of water daily, unless you also consume alcohol, then increase your water intake even more. The key to success: top every meal off with eight ounces of beef broth. Do you mind if I excuse myself? I'll be right back.

Somehow, I became the company's unofficial ear. I'd play confidante/psychiatrist to everyone who'd come see me with problems. I'd assure them that all their secrets would remain safe with me, because I could barely remember what these secrets were long enough to repeat them, even if I wanted to. Stuff like: *But she said she loved me, dammit, she swore.* And I'd listen and dispense the wise-sounding counsel of a condescending elder, as in *Welcome to reality, son. People say a lot of things; it's time to move on.*

This endless parade of advice seekers, with their mundane problems, turned out to be almost as draining and stressful as the HNC job, where the quantities I sold were measured by a daily, weekly, monthly, quarterly, and annual report card that documented the results.

One of the other VPs complained to me over lunch: As soon as you use a little brains around here, you get kicked in the ass. Then he looked at me sharply. Some of us do, anyway. And excuse my French.

I thought it odd, but Marshall dispatched me to South Africa as part of a delegation to drum up new business. It was good to get away from the nut factory headquarters, if only for a week. Before I even got back, though, it came to light: a blurry picture of me appearing to do some questionable things with a baboon. Something of dubious legality in every state but Wyoming.

My beloved and I shared another calm conversation around the dinner table.

The Internet makes mistakes sometimes, I told her, it's not infallible. People are out to get me, you're aware of that, right? There's this thing called Photo Shop you may have heard of. Look, most of my Fullmer colleagues are so jealous that they banded together and marched into Marshall's office to inform him that his shiny new toy, which would be me, is all surface glitter, and that the supposed work that I do doesn't amount to a damn thing. So, guess who's on top of his thing-a-ma-bob list now? The big guy called me in today with an ultimatum: I better come up with a solid plan to start earning my keep instead of just surfing the web all day. Or else.

*Wah!* my wife said. *Wah-wah!*

Never mind that, I told her. How long do you think I'll have to pretend, before it's safe to go back again and just do nothing?

# THE PAPERBOY INCIDENT
Frank Morelli

Humanity is a funny thing. We give ourselves this spunky, collective nickname to make us feel better. To fool ourselves into thinking we are more civilized than the mindless, drooling apes from which we sprung. But we all know it's mere illusion because, when it comes down to it, humans, like most other organisms, are self-serving creatures. We do stupid things to fulfill our singular, personal desires. The Cold War? The Crusades? That time you kissed your best friend's girlfriend? No different than a black bear with his paw stuck in a beehive, or two antelopes colliding headfirst in a grassy meadow. The motivations are the same. So, I guess that means the humanity of an individual—either man or beast—is strictly determined by how far one will go to achieve the desired end.

I was introduced to this brutal truth at an early age—seven years old, to be exact. The summer of 1985. Ronald Reagan was trickling it down in the oval office. *Back to the Future* was capitalizing on the stardom of one Alex P. Keaton from *Family Ties*. My shorts were barely longer than the tips of my fingers.

But something much more important was bubbling beneath the surface—the launch of a revolutionary new arcade game, one curiously missing the traditional joystick and two-button gameplay system of the behemoths of its day (like Donkey Kong and Pac-Man and Centipede). This new game was barely a game at all. It was more of a profession—or, at least, as far as I could foresee in my seven years on the planet. It stood tall in its particleboard cabinet with a teenage bike rider decaled on the side, his yellow hat flipped backwards and a devilish grin on his lips. A pair of handlebars with real BMX grips and functioning handbrakes reflected tiny flashes of light from the video screen, while digitized music backed by a drum machine blasted from a pair of onboard speakers.

That game was the Atari classic, *Paperboy*.

Okay, so I knew the thing wasn't reality. But it was cool. There was no denying it. And I figured, hey, if I was too young to deliver actual newspapers to my actual neighbors, at least I could gun a few cartoon newspapers through the pixelated windows of some unfortunate slobs in an imaginary town. All I needed was an in—one that would somehow fool my parents into thinking they'd actually enjoy spending any amount of time inside the cavernous walls of an arcade.

"It's still kind of early," I heard Mom whisper to Dad as we piled into our 1978 Volvo 240 Series, burgundy with camel-colored seats. We were on vacation in Wildwood, NJ, and had just finished a glorious round of putt-putt at Duffer's in the Crest. The place was always packed with family types—the moms still sporting their summer maternity clothes and pushing whining babies around in strollers, and the dads grumbling as they tried to figure out how their beer-guzzling and motorcycle-riding had swiftly morphed into diaper-changing and rounds of miniature golf on Friday nights.

The place boasted an ice cream parlor straight out of the Roaring 20s, and there was a small arcade around back. A really small arcade. So small there was never any room for the newest, most cutting-edge games of the day. All they had were a couple of pinball machines with stupid clowns or circus themes—like I was walking into some two-year-olds nursery. That's not what I was looking for. I was looking for *Paperboy*, and to find it I'd have to lure Mom and Dad to one of Wildwood's lowliest places, the 26th Street Arcade. Jonny's Arcade. On the Boardwalk. Where teenage girls in low-cut tops welcomed grubby hands in the back pockets of their jean shorts. Where gangly young men with patchy facial hair stacked coins on the ledges of pool tables and exhaled puffs of cigarette smoke in the density of storm clouds.

My parents would never go for it. That is, unless I could come up with the craftiest of diversions.

"I could go for some Curly's Fries," I blurted out, trying to strike while the iron was hot. I knew Mom and Dad were suckers for the Jersey Shore's premier French fry joint, which was nothing more than a five by ten hut on the side of the tramway tracks. Bags of russet potatoes and fresh lemons hung in burlap bags from the rafters, and you could stand outside and watch your fries and lemonade squashed, cut, and squeezed to perfection from scratch.

"Curly's?" Dad asked. "We ate two hours ago. What, do you have a tapeworm?"

"Frank! Don't say that." Mom, the ever-protective master of censorship, somehow thought my pristine eardrums were no match for even the least derogatory comment. Dad would grumble stuff under his breath and squeeze his Tom Selleck mustache between his thumb and forefinger when she shut him down like this. "We can definitely go to Curly's, Frankie. There's always room for fries."

"I thought that was dessert," Dad grumbled. "There's always room for—"

"Shut up, Frank. We're going to Curly's."

The plan was in motion. Now all I had to do was take advantage of the French fry coma Mom and Dad would drop into after consuming no less than twenty-two thousand calories.

We placed an order at one window—three large lemonades and a family bucket of fries—and watched our ingredients squish and slosh through gears and corkscrews and presses. Then the whole mess popped out in all its fast-food glory at another window a few feet away. Dad grabbed the cardboard bucket and his gallon of lemonade and Mom passed mine down to me. We sat at a picnic table on the edge of the boardwalk and listened to the waves whisper. And we smothered ourselves with French fries, never once stopping to breathe in the mixture of fresh sea air and spent peanut oil that hung over the pier or to wince at the searing lash of hot oil scorching the roofs of our mouths.

About the only things that could break my trance at that moment were the ringing bells and clickety-clack of the ticket dispenser on a nearby Skee-Ball game. Or the muffled pops and bops of a mallet aimed squarely at one of those pesky moles on the Whac-A-Mole. Or the flashing, Edison-style light bulbs that hung in the front window of Jonny's Arcade. With Dad's hand digging deeper and deeper in the fry bucket, I knew the time was now or never.

"How about I treat you both to a few games," I said, surprising even myself for a moment. Then I collected myself and I thought of this Mafia boss I'd seen in some gangster movie my Dad was always watching. He never seemed excited about anything, like if he just found out he won the lottery or if he found out his house had exploded it was all the same. So I continued like him, all suave-like. "You know…over at Jonny's. The arcade." I finished it off with a flourish of raised eyebrows and a final vibrating slurp of lemonade that bottomed out the cup.

Mom was first to respond. "You drink that lemonade too fast and you're gonna have to pee, Frankie. Do you have to pee? Because we can take you to—"

"Mom!" This wasn't the moment of triumph I had expected, and the moment was being shared with half the boardwalk. "No, Mom. I don't have to pee. I'm fine. I just want to play a game in there."

"And you're treating us?" Dad said through a mouth full of fries. "This I have to see."

"So we can go?"

"No," Mom said. "We're not going in that place. Would

you look at it, Frank?" Dad barely raised his eyes from the fry bucket. "You should have played one of the games at Duffer's."

"The stupid clown game? It's for babies."

"I seem to remember, just a few years ago, having to carry you out of that carnival at the first sight of a clown. I don't know why all of the sudden—"

"All right, all right." Thankfully, Dad always knew when to come to the rescue. He made me sweat a little, but he never let me roast. "You can go and play your game. One game. And then we're heading back to Uncle John and Aunt Jo's."

I knew enough not to say a word at that moment because Dad was famous for changing his mind at the drop of a hat. I reached into the pocket of my Wranglers and jangled around all the loose quarters I had saved since my birthday—which amounted to six, a nice haul. Then I popped up from the picnic table and took Dad's hand for our trek across the boardwalk. The air was warm and sticky, and the boards were bustling with enough people for two Saturday nights. Dad guided me through a tangle of arms and feet and strollers and shopping bags. At one point, he threw an arm across my chest and halted me as a moving tramcar blared its automated message in my ear—*Watch the tramcar, please!*

All the bouncing around and sidestepping made one thing rapidly apparent: Mom was right. I had to pee. All the signs were there. Weird sloshing sound in my stomach? Check. Odd compulsion to dance around uncontrollably? Check. Pressure and discomfort in the unmentionable area? Double check. But Jonny's was in sight, and the electric glow of an imaginary paper route beckoned me forth.

When we reached the entrance, Dad stopped walking. He gave a scrutinizing look to a teenage boy in a leather jacket with all sorts of patches stitched to it. Then he knelt down in front of me. "I think this is something you can handle on your own, sport. You made your pitch like a man, now it's time you finish the job like one."

I didn't know how to respond. It was the first time Dad was letting me go out on my own. He trusted me to take care of myself. If Mom were here, I thought, she'd kill him. It was the coolest thing I'd ever seen my dad do, up to that point. So, I knew I had to take him up on the offer.

"Go ahead," he said. "I'll be right here."

Without thinking, I pushed straight ahead, through the open-air entrance at Jonny's, and into the thick of the arcade. Plumes of cigarette smoke swirled in the dim light like wayward ghosts, illuminated only by flashes from the video screens. And, amid the darkness, like a pillar of light rising up from the cavernous floor, was my holy grail.

I ducked and dodged my way over to it with an ocean's worth of lemonade still sloshing around down below, and I had my quarters out and nearly in the slots when a thick hand wrapped in a studded leather bracelet gripped me by the wrist. I looked up into the face of a bearded teenage ogre, replete with oozing pimples and mangled teeth. The stench of rotten fish heads trailed from his mouth when he spoke.

"There's a line here, rug rat. Didn't your mommy tell you about them?"

His grip on my wrist grew a little tighter. A little too tight, if you must know. And I saw my Dad moving a few steps closer to the entrance. I grabbed my quarters and backed off, and Dad let me do my thing, which was to haul myself to the back of a line that snaked its way through half the arcade and ended somewhere near the air hockey tables.

The farther I walked, the heavier my stomach felt, and the more I had to strain to prevent the inevitable. My perch at the end of the line was somewhere in the range of Tanzania. I could barely see *Paperboy* from there, let alone play it. But I had come all this way, and Dad was watching. There was no way I was going to let something as meaningless and stupid as my bladder prevent me from glory.

So I waited.

Ten minutes became twenty.

Twenty became a half hour.

The line moved a few feet at a time, until I could almost make out the writing on the side of the game panel. All the while, and unbeknownst to me, my kidneys continued to process molecule after sweet molecule of Curly's lemonade, depositing it drop by drop in my bladder until it was roughly the size of the Hindenburg.

About forty minutes into the excursion, I was dancing out of my socks. There were only three people in front of me in line, and I could see Dad scoping me from the entrance. I started to count down from twenty. Anything to keep my mind off of my bladder. *Twenty…nineteen…eighteen…seventeen…* I looked to my right and a gamer sliced through the waves on a robotic jet ski. Water splashed and trickled and spilled all around him on screen. *Twenty-nineteen-eighteen…* I looked to my left and a girl with silver bangles the size of hula hoops guzzled from a glass Pepsi bottle. *Twentynineteeneighteen…* I looked straight ahead and noticed the arcade manager approached the machine. He's taking out a key. He's opening up the safe. This may take a while. I'm dancing some more. I'll burst before I make it to that machine. I'll never get there. But I have to. Dad is watching and I want to play the game. But it's too late.

The patrons in Jonny's Arcade have already jumped back to form a semi-circle around me, and the warmth is spreading across the front of my jeans, leaving the denim darker and bluer in its wake. There's a trickling sound down near my feet where liquid drips from the bottom of my pant legs and patters on the concrete floor, and in the background, I hear that squiggly sound Pac-Man makes when he runs head first into one of those red, goblin-looking guys. Then a shadow looms over me, followed by the clinking of change. The manager.

"What the hell are you doing, kid?" His voice was low and snarling, and his bushy eyebrows twitched around on his face like a pair of angry squirrels. "What the hell is this?" I was frozen in time, unable to move or breathe or speak or do much of anything. "Is this piss, kid? Well, is it?" There were a few muffled laughs from the spectators. "Well are you gonna say something or are you just gonna piss and run?"

All I could think to say was, "I just got done swimming in the ocean. Can't you see that?"

I doubt the gangster guy from my dad's movie would have been impressed. Neither were the spectators in Jonny's Arcade, for that matter. They howled and laughed and wagged their fingers at me until I felt a different warmth welling up. This time behind my eyes. Believe me, the last thing I wanted was to be bawling and standing in a puddle of my own urine next to the best video game I've never played. But that's how it happened—at least, until Dad swooped in and carried me off to the sanctuary of my Aunt and Uncle's shore house.

He always lets me sweat but never roast.

The next day, I just wanted to forget about everything—about embarrassing myself in front of everyone at the arcade; about trying to outsmart my parents; about that stupid game, *Paperboy*, altogether. But kids often have a way of finding out needless information, and such was the case with my gangrenous group of goofy cousins. They'd somehow found out about my little incident at the arcade—presumably before the first drop had even hit the floor—and they were primed to spend the entire day on the beach reminding me of the fact.

Thus came the nickname "Frankie Pee-Pee Pants," which they used ad nauseum as we rode body boards and built sandcastles and played paddleball. You'd think they would have come up with a better name. Maybe add a touch of alliteration in there for good measure, like "Flowing Frankie" or "Frankie Fire Hydrant." "Frankie Pee-Pee Pants" is what they went with.

But that wasn't the worst of it. The worst came in the form of outright slander. And my oldest cousin, Joseph, was the primary culprit.

"This is my cousin, Frank," he said to a girl as we pressed wet sand into mud castles at the water's edge. There was something about this girl, in her pink one-piece and her straw hat. She reminded me of the girl on the Coppertone bottle. It was the first time I ever entertained the thought that girls might not be so icky after all. Then my stupid cousin opened his fat yap one more time. "He peed his pants in the middle of the arcade last night."

And that was that. Coppertone girl shook her head, grabbed her plastic bucket, and went in search of more refined mud castle builders. But, before she was out of earshot, I thought of pulling the old gangster routine one more time. Maybe a little something to hit my idiot cousin right where it hurt most. Something like, "Yeah, those rubber sheets you have on your mattress aren't that mysterious there, cuz."

But I didn't. Because I guess we all have a line we won't cross…even to get the things we want most. Even when we're seven years old.

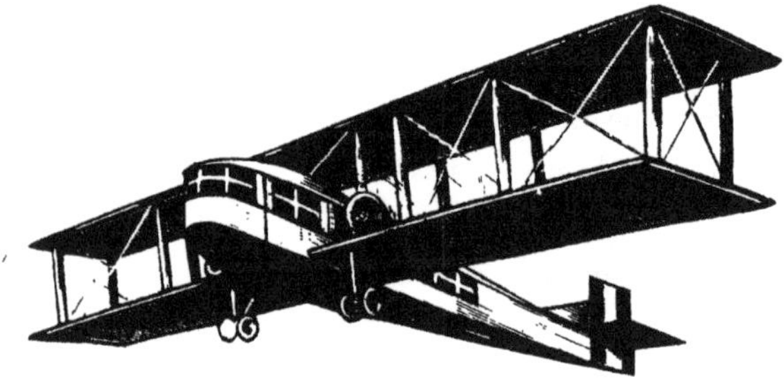

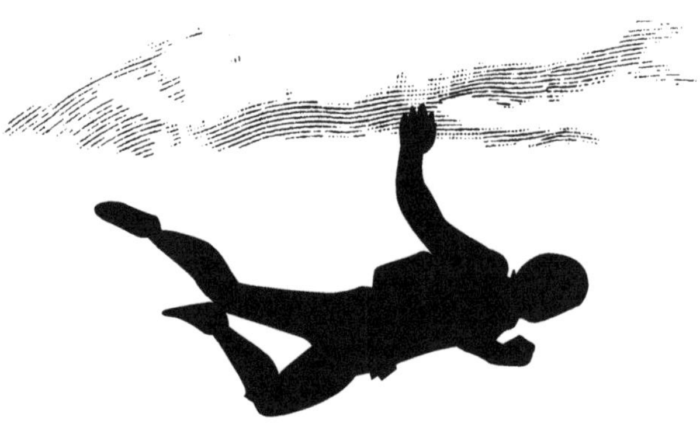

# CONTRIBUTORS

**Rob Dinsmoor** is the author of three fictive memoirs, *Tales of the Troupe*, *The Yoga Divas and Other Stories*, and *You Can Leave Anytime*. He also co-authored a children's picture book titled *Does Dixie Like Me?* His story in *Lowestoft Chronicle*, 'Kundalini Yoga at the Arkham YMCA,' was nominated for a Pushcart Prize. Recently, he appeared on stage on The Moth Story Slam. He lives on the North Shore of Massachusetts. Website www.robertdinsmoor.com.

**Nicholas Litchfield** is the founding editor of *Lowestoft Chronicle* and author of the suspense novel *Swampjack Virus*. He has worked in various countries as a tabloid journalist, librarian, and media researcher. He writes regularly for the *Colorado Review* and his book reviews for the *Lancashire Post* are syndicated to twenty-five newspapers across the UK. He lives in western New York. Roam his website at www.nicholaslitchfield.com.

**Arianna S. Warsaw-Fan Rauch** is a freelance violinist and writer. In the years directly following her graduation from Juilliard, she recorded an album with Grammy-award-winning label Sono Luminus, collaborated with such notable artists as Christopher Plummer, Sir James Galway, and Chris Botti, and performed in venues across the world—from The Kennedy Center and Boston Symphony Hall to Milan's Sala Verdi and the Newport Performing Arts Theater in Manila. At the age of twenty-eight, after earning approximately one quarter of the amount that her parents had previously invested in her musical training, she felt entitled to enter a phase of semi-retirement in order to pursue her passion for writing. Now she is rarely employed, but she is busy nevertheless—consumed by futile, narcissistic endeavors which are considered worthwhile only by her (and members of her immediate family). Her writing has appeared in *The Satirist*, *The Higgs Weldon*, and *Bustle*. She lives in Berlin, Germany with her remarkably tolerant husband, who enables her delusions by laughing at everything she writes, applauding loudly whenever she plays the violin, and working at a real job so that she, along with their eventual vizslas and children, can have food and shelter.

Author/speaker **Mary Beth Magee**'s faith leads her to explore God's world and write about it. She writes news, reviews and feature articles for print and online publications; cozy Christian fiction, poetry, and devotions, as well as recollections in several anthologies. Her monthly newsletter includes a free short story. Visit her website at www.LOL4.net.

During his academic career, Dr. **Sheldon Russell** authored twenty-five professional articles and co-authored the text, *An Interdisciplinary Approach to Reading and Mathematics*. He retired as Professor Emeritus from the University of Central Oklahoma in 2000. He has had ten novels published: *Empire*, a suspense novel; two historic frontier novels, *The Savage Trail* and *Requiem at Dawn*; *Dreams to Dust: A Tale of the Oklahoma Land Rush*; *The Dig: In Search of Coronado's Treasure*; and the Hook Runyon mystery series (*The Yard Dog*, *The Insane Train*, *Dead Man's Tunnel*, *The Hanging of Samuel Ash*, and *The Bridge Troll Murders*). He and his wife currently reside on their home ranch in northwestern Oklahoma, where they both work daily at their respective crafts. Russell enjoys reading, gardening, and collecting his favorite books.

**Sharon Frame Gay** grew up a child of the highway, playing by the side of the road. She has been internationally published in many anthologies as well as *Gravel, BioStories, Crannóg Magazine, Luna Luna, Fiction on the Web, Literary Orphans*, and others. She is a Pushcart Prize nominee.

**Michael C. Keith** is the author of more than 20 books on electronic media. In addition, he is the author of an acclaimed memoir, *The Next Better Place*; a young adult novel, *Life is Falling Sideways*; and eleven story collections—*Of Night and Light, Everything is Epic, Sad Boy, And Through the Trembling Air, Hoag's Object, The Collector of Tears, If Things Were Made To Last Forever, Caricatures, The Near Enough, Bits, Specks, Crumbs, Flecks*, and *Slow Transit*. He has been nominated five times for a Pushcart Prize and was a finalist for the National Indie Excellence Award for short fiction anthology and a finalist for the 2013 International Book Award in the "Fiction Visionary" category. Website www.michaelckeith.com.

**Todd McKie** is an artist and writer who staggers, paint-spattered and dazed, between canvas and keyboard. His stories have appeared in *PANK, Chicago Literati*, STORY, *McSweeney's Internet Tendency*, and elsewhere. Todd lives in Boston and blogs sporadically at toddmckie.blogspot.com.

**Tamra Plotnick**'s poetry and prose works have been published in a number of journals and anthologies, including *Serving House Journal*; *The Waiting Room Reader, Vol II: Words to Keep You Company*, edited by Rachel Hadas; and *Global City Review: International Edition*. She teaches high school in New York City and lives in Brooklyn with her husband, son, and daughter.

**Robert Mangeot** lives in Nashville, Tennessee with his wife and cats. His short fiction appears here and there, including *Alfred Hitchcock Mystery Magazine*, *Lowestoft Chronicle*, the Anthony-winning *Murder Under the Oaks* and *The Oddville Press*. When not writing, he can be found wandering the snack food aisles of America or France.

**Charles Joseph Albert** works in a metallurgy shop in San Jose, California, where he lives with his wife and three boys. He has been interested in writing ever since the third grade when he had to learn Frost's "Runaway." His poems and fiction have appeared recently in *The Literary Nest, Quarterday, Chicago Literati, 300 Days of Sun, Abstract Jam, The Literary Hatchet,* and *Here Comes Everyone.*

**Jill Hawkins** is a recent graduate student of the Red Earth MFA program at Oklahoma City University. She was born and raised in Oklahoma. She has publications of poems in *JAMA: Journal of the American Medical Association and Blacktop Passages,* as well is in *Southwestern American Literature, Pink.Girl.Ink., Poeming Pigeon, Mizna, The Dragon Poet Review,* and *The Endeavor.*

A senior lecturer at San José State University and ethnoecologist focusing on biocultural diversity, Dr. **Jeanine Pfeiffer** has published meta-analyses in major scientific journals and edited volumes on conservation. A finalist in the 2016 Hunger Mountain creative nonfiction contest, her Pushcart-prize nominated prose has appeared in the *Bellevue Literary Review, Hippocampus, Nowhere, Between the Lines,* and *Langscape*. More at www.jeaninepfeiffer.com.

**Kenneth P. Gurney** lives in Albuquerque, NM, USA. His latest collection of poems is *Stump Speech*. He now edits the poetry blog *Watermelon Isotope*. His personal website is kpgurney.me.

Born with the eye of a writer and the heart of a storyteller, **Karen Fayeth**'s work is colored by the Mexican, Native American, and Western influences of her roots in rural New

Mexico and complemented by an evolving urban aesthetic. Now living in the San Francisco Bay area, she can be found online at karenfayeth.com.

**Robert Wexelblatt** is professor of humanities at Boston University's College of General Studies. He has published the story collections *Petites Suites*, *Life in the Temperate Zone*, *The Decline of Our Neighborhood*, *The Artist Wears Rough Clothing*, and *Heiberg's Twitch*; a book of essays, *Professors at Play*; two short novels, *Losses* and *The Derangement of Jules Torquemal*, and essays, stories, and poems in a variety of scholarly and literary journals. His novel *Zublinka Among Women* won the Indie Book Awards first-place prize for fiction. A collection of essays, *The Posthumous Papers of Sidney Fein*, is forthcoming.

**Lenny Levine** attended Brooklyn College, graduating in 1962 with a BA in Speech and Theater. Immediately thereafter, he forgot about all of that and became a folk singer, then a folk-rock singer and songwriter, and finally a studio singer and composer of many successful jingles, including McDonald's, Lipton Tea, and Jeep. Levine composed songs and sang backup for Billy Joel, Neil Diamond, Peggy Lee, Diana Ross, Barry Manilow, the Pointer Sisters, Carly Simon, and others. In addition, he performed for a number of years with the improvisational comedy group War Babies. His work has appeared in *Amarillo Bay*, *Bitter Oleander*, *Cairn*, *The Dirty Goat*, *Diverse Voices Quarterly*, *Eleven Eleven*, *Forge*, *The Griffin*, *Hobo Pancakes*, *The Jabberwock Review*, *Rio Grande Review*, *RiverSedge*, *Rougarou*, *Verdad*, *Westview*, and *Wild Violet*. He received a 2011 Pushcart Prize nomination for short fiction.

**James B. Nicola**'s poems have appeared three times in *Lowestoft Chronicle*, as well as in the *Antioch*, *Southwest* and *Atlanta Reviews*, *Rattle*, *Tar River*, and *Poetry East*. A Yale grad, he won a Dana

Literary Award, a People's Choice award (from Storyteller) and a Willow Review award; he was nominated twice for a Pushcart Prize and once for a Rhysling Award, and he was a featured poet at New Formalist. His nonfiction book *Playing the Audience* won a Choice award. His two poetry collections, published by Word Poetry, are *Manhattan Plaza* (2014) and *Stage to Page: Poems from the Theater* (2016). *Out of Nothing: Poems of Art and Artists* is available from Shanti Arts. More at sites.google.com/site/jamesbnicola.

Once a professor of French literature, **Mary Donaldson-Evans** came down out of the ivory tower in 2011 and hasn't looked back. Her creative work has been published by *The New York Times* ("Metropolitan Diary"), *The Stir@CafeMom*, the *Lowestoft Chronicle*, *Diverse Voices Quarterly*, *Corner Club Quarterly* and *BoomerLitMag*.

**Alistair Rey** is a writer of fiction and parafiction who currently resides in Cardiff, Wales. In the past, his work has appeared in such magazines as the *Parenthetical Review* and *Juked*, among other publications.

**Scott Dominic Carpenter** teaches literature and creative writing at Carleton College (MN). He is the author of *Theory of Remainders: A Novel* (named to Kirkus Reviews' "Best Books of 2013") and *This Jealous Earth: Stories*. His shorter work has appeared in a wide variety of venues, including *South Dakota Review*, *The Rumpus*, *Silk Road*, and various anthologies. His website is sdcarpenter.com.

**George Moore**'s collections include *Saint Agnes Outside the Walls* (FutureCycle 2016) and *Children's Drawings of the Universe* (Salmon Poetry 2015). Nominated for six Pushcart Prizes, and a finalist for both the National Poetry Series and the Brittingham Poetry Award, his work has appeared in *The Atlantic*, *Arc*, *Orbis*, *Poetry*, *Valparaiso* and *Lowestoft Chronicle*. He lives with his wife on the south shore of Nova Scotia.

**Elaine Barnard** has traveled extensively. Her short stories have been published in numerous literary journals, such as *Lowestoft Chronicle*, *Anak Sastra*, *Mandala*, *Diverse Voices*, *Apple Valley*, and many others. She has been a finalist for Glimmer Train and Best of the Net. She received her MFA from the University of California, Irvine. Currently, she is at work on a collection of her short travel stories.

**Sabrina Harris** is a fiction writer now based in Brooklyn after years spent living and working in Sweden, France, Lithuania and Serbia. She is currently working on her first novel, *Afterbirth*.

**Roland Barnes** published poetry when he was young. Early in a career in psychiatric social work, he placed an article in an extinct English journal *Community Medicine*, which re-established his interest in writing, becoming a regular contributor to health, housing, and social services magazines. More recently, he has published in *The Oldie*, and *Best of Britain* magazines and is currently working on two full-length manuscripts: *In Place of Cotton*, a childhood in Oldham, and *The English House*, about living in north Portugal. After living in London with his family for most of his life, they have recently moved to Swansea, South Wales, around the corner from Dylan Thomas's birthplace.

**Saundra Norton** received her MFA in poetry from Sarah Lawrence College where she is currently the director of the Child Development Institute. She has lived in Paris where she followed in the footsteps of expatriate writers and hiked the Camino de Santiago across Spain. She cat-sat in Prague for two summers where she attended the Prague Summer Seminars and gave poetry readings to mainly Czech-speaking audiences. She serves as a US representative for World Organization for Early Childhood Education/Organisation Mondiale pour l'Education Prescolaire (OMEP)'s UN Economic and Social Council (ECOSOC).

**Anthony Head** is a writer and editor based in Tokyo. His articles have appeared in numerous journals, including *Edinburgh Review*, *The London Magazine*, *History Today*, *Far Eastern Economic Review*, *The Global Dispatches* and *The Times Literary Supplement* (TLS). He is the editor of three volumes of the letters and diaries of John Cowper Powys, and two collections of essays by Llewelyn Powys. He is currently working on a collection of his own Japan-related essays and articles.

**Richard Luftig** is a former professor of educational psychology and special education at Miami University in Ohio, now residing in California. He is a recipient of the Cincinnati Post-Corbett Foundation Award for Literature and a semi-finalist for the Emily Dickinson Society Award. His poems have appeared in numerous literary journals in the United States and internationally in Japan, Canada, Australia, Europe, Thailand, Hong Kong and India.

**Tushar Jain** was the winner of the 2012 Srinivas Rayaprol Poetry Prize, 2013 Poetry with Prakriti Prize, 2014 RL Poetry Award, 2014 DWL Short Story Contest, and 2016 Toto Funds the Arts Award for Creative Writing. His work is published in various literary magazines and journals, such as *aaduna, Papercuts, The Nervous Breakdown, Antiserious, RaedLeaf Poetry India, Young Ravens Literary Review, Lowestoft Chronicle, The Madras Mag, Coldnoon, Streetcake Magazine, Sierra Nevada Review, Into the Void Magazine, The Cape Rock, Miracle, Dryland, The Bookends Review, Edify Fiction, Gramma, decomP, Priestess & Hierophant*

*Press*, *Barking Sycamores*, *Literary Heist*, *The Wax Paper*, *The Wagon Magazine*. He lives and works in Mumbai.

**Olga Pavlinova Olenich** is a widely published writer from Australia.

**Judy S. Richardson** lives in Richmond, Virginia. As a professor of Education, she wrote numerous articles for academic journals as well as three textbooks. She received the Virginia Commonwealth University Award of Excellence, the Association of Literacy Educators & Researchers Laureate Award, and two Fulbright Scholar awards. The professional articles she enjoyed writing most were in narrative style, so she could focus on the story behind the research. Currently, she is writing short stories, memoir, and fiction. She has been published in *The Penmen Review* and *Persimmon Tree*.

**Joe Albanese** is a writer from South Jersey. He graduated from Rowan University, where he majored in Law and Justice. His work can be found in 2017 issues of *Burningword Literary Journal*, *Calliope*, *Kansas City Voices*, *Steel Toe Review*, and other publications.

**Brennen Fahy** spends his summers fighting wildfires which allows him to pursue an interest in traveling and writing during the winter. His work has appeared in *The Globe and Mail* and the *Lowestoft Chronicle*. He received his degree from the University of Victoria and currently resides in Vancouver, British Columbia.

**Ruyi Wen** writes short stories from a quiet suburb in Texas, where she lives with her husband, daughter, and their menagerie of well-behaved houseplants.

**Dietrich Kalteis** is the award-winning author of *Ride the Lightning, The Deadbeat Club, Triggerfish, House of Blazes* and *Zero Avenue*. Nearly fifty of his short stories have been published internationally, and he lives with his family on Canada's west coast.

Since 2015, **AN Block**'s stories have appeared in *Buffalo Almanack* (recipient of its Inkslinger Award for Creative Excellence), *Umbrella Factory Magazine* (a 2016 Pushcart Prize nominee), *The Maine Review, New Pop Lit, Falling Star, DenimSkin, Per Contra, Burningwood Literary Journal, Crack The Spine, Constellations, The Bicycle Review, Lakeview International Journal of Literature and Arts, Flash Frontier, Foliate Oak Literary Magazine, Down in the Dirt, Contrary*, the *Blue Bonnet Review, The Nite Writers Literary Arts Journal, Lowestoft Chronicle* (a 2017 Pushcart Prize nominee), and *The Binnacle*, the latter of which won Honorable Mention in its Twelfth and Thirteenth Annual International Ultra-Short Competitions. He has an MA in History and is a Master of Wine, who teaches at Boston University. He is also a contributing editor at the *Improper Bostonian*.

**Frank Morelli** plucked his roots from the cozy, northern soil and buried them in the sunbaked clays of North Carolina. His work has appeared in *Philadelphia Stories, Cobalt, Change Seven Magazine, Jersey Devil Press, East Coast Literary Review, Rind, Lowestoft Chronicle*, and *Scarlet Leaf Review*.

# COPYRIGHT NOTES

"On the Oxford to York," copyright © 2017 by Arianna S. Warsaw-Fan Rauch. First published in Lowestoft Chronicle, issue #29.

"Traveling Companion," copyright © 2017 by Mary Beth Magee. First published in Lowestoft Chronicle, issue #29.

"The Return of the Railroad Bull: A Conversation with Sheldon Russell," copyright © 2018 by Lowestoft Chronicle. First published in Lowestoft Chronicle, issue #33.

"One Star," copyright © 2017 by Sharon Frame Gay. First published in Lowestoft Chronicle, issue #31.

"Sarge," copyright © 2016 by Michael C. Keith. First published in Lowestoft Chronicle, issue #25.

"Rome 1973," copyright © 2017 by Todd McKie. First published in Lowestoft Chronicle, issue #30.

"Chariot," copyright © 2017 by Tamra Plotnick. First published in Lowestoft Chronicle, issue #31.

"La Tomatina," copyright © 2017 by Robert Mangeot. First published in Lowestoft Chronicle, issue #31.

"Angie's Wedding," © 2017 by Charles Joseph Albert. First published in Lowestoft Chronicle, issue #32.

"R.O.T. Rallies," copyright © 2017 by Jill Hawkins. First published in Lowestoft Chronicle, issue #30.

"Bite Me," copyright © 2017 by Jeanine Pfeiffer. First published in Lowestoft Chronicle, issue #29.

"Manna," copyright © 2017 by Kenneth P. Gurney. First published in Lowestoft Chronicle, issue #29.

"Holy Water," copyright © 2017 by Karen Fayeth. First published in Lowestoft Chronicle, issue #32.

"Hsi-Wei and the Good," © 2017 by Robert Wexelblatt. First published in Lowestoft Chronicle, issue #31.

"Whose Fault?," copyright © 2017 by Lenny Levine. First published in Lowestoft Chronicle, issue #29.

"Strangers on a Train," copyright © 2017 by James B. Nicola. First published in Lowestoft Chronicle, issue #32.

"The Sweetest Sound," copyright © 2017 by Mary Donaldson-Evans. First published in Lowestoft Chronicle, issue #30.

"A World of Eternal Silence," copyright © 2017 by Alistair Rey. First published in Lowestoft Chronicle, issue #32.

"The Acute and the Grave," copyright © 2017 by Scott Dominic Carpenter. First published in Lowestoft Chronicle, issue #31.

"The Mystery of the Stairs," copyright © 2017 by George Moore. First published in Lowestoft Chronicle, issue #31.

"Emily," copyright © 2016 by Elaine Barnard. First published in Lowestoft Chronicle, issue #28.

"Massaged in Vein," copyright © 2017 by Sabrina Harris. First published in Lowestoft Chronicle, issue #29.

"What Do Mares Eat?," copyright © 2017 by Rob Dinsmoor. First published in Lowestoft Chronicle, issue #31.

"A Daihatsu Doctor," copyright © 2016 by Roland Barnes. First published in Lowestoft Chronicle, issue #26.

"The Taxi I Called," copyright © 2017 by Saundra Norton. First published in Lowestoft Chronicle, issue #30.

"Japanese Taxis and Elementary Incidents," copyright © 2017 by Anthony Head. First published in Lowestoft Chronicle, issue #30.

"Self-Portrait," copyright © 2017 by Richard Luftig. First published in Lowestoft Chronicle, issue #29.

"The Man With No Outlines," copyright © 2017 by Tushar Jain. First published in Lowestoft Chronicle, issue #32.

"Musical Chairs at Larksome Lodge," © 2016 by Olga Pavlinova Olenich. First published in Lowestoft Chronicle, issue #26.

"Lost and Found in Russia," copyright © 2017 by Judy S. Richardson. First published in Lowestoft Chronicle, issue #31.

"Hitchhiker," copyright © 2017 by Joe Albanese. First published in Lowestoft Chronicle, issue #31.

"The Vomit Comet To Koh Tao," copyright © 2017 by Brennen Fahy. First published in Lowestoft Chronicle, issue #30.

"Farmer Joe," copyright © 2017 by Ruyi Wen. First published in Lowestoft Chronicle, issue #32.

"Conversation with Dietrich Kalteis," copyright © 2017 by Lowestoft Chronicle. First published in Lowestoft Chronicle, issue #32.

"Dream Job," copyright © 2017 by AN Block. First published in Lowestoft Chronicle, issue #30.

"The Paperboy Incident," copyright © 2017 by Frank Morelli. First published in Lowestoft Chronicle, issue #30.

# ACKNOWLEDGEMENTS

With special thanks to Amie McLaughlin for her valuable feedback and for proofreading much of the prose in the magazine over the past six years. Special thanks also to Tara for her help with the magazine and her outstanding graphic design work, and to the wonderfully talented Rob Dinsmoor, Dietrich Kalteis, Robert Wexelblatt, and Sheldon Russell. The magazine wouldn't exist if it weren't for the marvelous contributors we've been fortunate to publish. Much gratitude to everyone who has contributed to the magazine.

**Bon Voyage!**

Other titles in the acclaimed anthology series!

# Lowestoft Chronicle 2011 Anthology
### Edited by Nicholas Litchfield

"This is a fine anthology that I found both provocative and enjoyable. Highest praise: it made me want to write short stories again."
—Luke Rhinehart, author of the cult classic *The Dice Man*

"Michael Connor's 'Stevie and Louie' is a fun read about a young, single tourist in Austin…'The Shooting Party' by Jack Frey is a story of a chance encounter in an exotic location that is both plausible and mysterious. It makes good use of dialogue and an inventive plot."
—*New York Journal of Books*

"All things considered, it might just be a very good thing if the Lowestoft Chronicle were to achieve their goal of world domination."
—Cheryl LaGuardia, *Library Journal*

# Far-flung and Foreign
### Edited by Nicholas Litchfield

"Hot off the press [is] this terrific anthology culled from Lowestoft Chronicle. The writing here is fresh, surprising, and alive. Not to be missed is the bittersweet interview with the author Augustine Funnell. (Please write more!) The book looks and feels great."
—Nicholas Rombes, author of *A Cultural Dictionary of Punk*

"Nicely laid out…eclectic…humorous pieces with an emphasis on travel, hence many of the works take one to far-away and exotic places. I immensely enjoyed 'The Adventures of Root Beer Float Man' by Michael Frissore. For poetry, try Wayne Lee's 'Ordinary Deckhand.'"
—*Newpages.com*

"I've enjoyed reading the *Chronicle*. 'I Like Your Deer's Moustache, and other Lithuanian Tales' …[is] a distinctly Baltic twist on mistaken identity. One of our most popular pieces."
—*My Audio Universe*
(Rijn Collin's story aired on the independent radio station KVMR)

To order, visit www.lowestoftchronicle.com

# Intrepid Travelers
### Edited by Nicholas Litchfield

"Without a single stinker or filler piece in the bunch. I was extremely impressed with the variety and quality of the writing. *Intrepid Travelers* is a solid collection of funny and fine travel-themed stories, poetry, essays and interviews that easily fits in a back pocket or carry-on bag."
—Frank Mundo, *Examiner.com*

"Many short stories and poems here offer deeper meanings and address heavier topics. 'Something Like Culture Shock' by Dennis Vanvick…[has] good character development and a compelling story. 'Political Awakening, 1970' by Denise Thompson-Slaughter…it was refreshing to read a piece with this much depth. 'Pájaro Diablo' by Michael C. Keith…by the end, the reader is riveted to see what will happen next. Also features an interview with Randal S. Brandt…[which] make[s] for an entertaining read. Overall, this is full of great talent and exceptionally written pieces."
—Tara Smith, *The Review Review*

"Refreshing and well-written, *Intrepid Travelers* takes the reader to a wide variety of literary destinations, and makes even a confirmed hermit like me want to get up and go somewhere. Highly recommended."
—James Reasoner, *Rough Edges*

"Prepare for an adrenalin surge as a thief tries to escape from armed Mafia agents in Hector S. Koburn's fatalistic 'Bloody Driving Gloves,' Steve Gronert Ellerhoff's brilliantly quirky short story, 'Apophallation,' [and] Michael C. Keith's unexpectedly moving 'Pájaro Diablo.' *Intrepid Travelers* is a coruscating cornucopia of humour, drama and big, beautiful adventures. Highly original and entertaining."
— Pam Norfolk, *Blackpool Gazette*

"It's unique and the quality of the writing is amazingly high."
—Luke Rhinehart, internationally bestselling author of *The Dice Man*

# Somewhere, Sometime...
### Edited by Nicholas Litchfield

"The latest collection of prose and poetry from the *Lowestoft Chronicle* is a genuine pleasure. Nicholas Litchfield has put together something very special, something to celebrate, enjoy, savor."
—Jay Parini, bestselling author of *The Last Station* and *Why Poetry Matters*

"What a lovely book. Well designed, thoughtfully laid out, and with a grand assortment of content."
—Matthew P. Mayo, Spur Award-winning author of *Tucker's Reckoning*

# Other Places
### Edited by NICHOLAS LITCHFIELD

"In the age of tweets and sound bites, it's heartening to read *Other Places*, a publication celebrating the power and beauty of a story well told."
—SHELDON RUSSELL, author of the Hook Runyon Mystery series

"*Other Places*, a mouth-watering feast of short stories, poems, narrative non-fiction, and in-depth interviews, is the latest anthology from the much-admired *Lowestoft Chronicle*, an eclectic and innovative online journal. Packed into the pages are stories to entice, enthral, and entertain. Litchfield also serves up a tasty blend of pleasing and deftly prepared poems. And if you still aren't sated by this literary banquet, tuck into Litchfield's incisive and enlightening interviews with three critically acclaimed, multitalented writers."
—PAM NORFOLK, *Wigan Evening Post*

"I really loved the latest anthology from Lowestoft, *Other Places*. It's a brilliant, savory, sharp, amusing and varied taste of my favorite magazine, *Lowestoft Chronicle*. I'm delighted that a place exists for this kind of travel writing—if that's a term for it. And it's not a good one. This is just great writing about place, ranging from the spirit of place to the human spirit. Go anywhere with Lowestoft. And enjoy the trip."
—JAY PARINI, internationally bestselling author of *The Passages of H.M.*

"*Other Places* is the usual delightful mix of stories, poems, author interviews, and non-fiction gleaned from the pages of the *Lowestoft Chronicle*, the only literary magazine I read on a regular basis. Always entertaining and insightful, *Other Places* is well worth your time, whether you're a veteran traveler or a hermit like me!"
—JAMES REASONER, *Rough Edges*

"Armchair travelers, rejoice! Editor Nicholas Litchfield has released *Lowestoft Chronicle*'s anthology for summer 2015, *Other Places*. Filled with fiction, nonfiction and poetry about travel and destinations, the book brings the far corners of the world to the reader's armchair. The stories and poems vary in tone from dead serious to delightful whimsy, offering something for every taste. Humor, adventure and mystery share the pages with intriguing result."
—MARY BETH MAGEE, *Examiner.com*

"Sick of fly-by journalism and travel dilettantes? The antidote is *Lowestoft Chronicle*'s most recent anthology, *Other Places*—a collection of essays, stories, and poetry devoted to the in-depth experience of culture. Whether humorous, touching, or revelatory, these expertly curated pieces throw you in contact with the real."
—SCOTT DOMINIC CARPENTER, author of *Theory of Remainders*

**To order, visit www.lowestoftchronicle.com**

# Grand Departures

Edited by NICHOLAS LITCHFIELD
Foreword by Robert Garner McBrearty

"The stories, poems, and essays in Nicholas Litchfield's latest anthology, *Grand Departures*, are haunting, idiosyncratic, and unexpected, like the true delights of travel."
—IVY GOODMAN, award-winning author of *Heart Failure*

"A must-have collection of travelers' delights and demons."
—NANCY CARONIA, contributor to *Somewhere, Sometime* and co-editor of *Personal Effects*

"An impressive collection of travel works that sweeps the reader across the globe."
—DORENE O'BRIEN, award-winning author of *Voices of the Lost and Found*

"It is fun, edgy at times, international in its scope. It surprises. The work is a blend of the serious and the comical, dark shades, light shades, and as I said, ever surprising."
—ROBERT GARNER MCBREARTY, author of *The Western Lonesome Society*

# Invigorating Passages

Edited by NICHOLAS LITCHFIELD
Foreword by Matthew P. Mayo

"A powerful literary passport—this adventurous anthology is all stamped up with exciting travel-themed writing. With humor, darkness, and charm, its lively prose and poetry will drop you into memorable physical and psychological landscapes. Pack your bags!"
—JOSEPH SCAPELLATO, acclaimed author of *Big Lonesome*

"A wonderful collection from a fine literary journal. Fine writing that stirs the imagination, often amuses and always entertains."
—DIETRICH KALTEIS, award-winning author of *Ride the Lightning*

"*Invigorating Passages* delivers on all counts, hits on all cylinders too. The writing is skilled, the choices rich, the passages manifold, and the invigoration unfailing."
—ROBERT WEXELBLATT, award-winning author of *Zublinka Among Women*

"*Invigorating Passages* is a rare and dynamic literary collection which grabs readers firmly and sweeps them away to strange and exhilarating places, presenting intriguing situations, colourful characters, and making us yearn to strap on the backpack and go exploring."
—PAM NORFOLK, *Lancashire Post*

To order, visit www.lowestoftchronicle.com

CPSIA information can be obtained
at www.ICGtesting.com
Printed in the USA
LVHW03s1217091018
592959LV00001B/10/P

9 781732 332805